Unleashing your potential

A journey to personal mastery

By

Laurie F. Kimberly

Copyright

All rights reserved, no part of this publication may be reproduced, distributed or transmitted in any form or by any means, including photocopying, recording or other electronic or mechanical methods, without the prior written permission of the publisher, except in case of brief quotations embodied in critical reviews and certain other non commercial uses permitted by copyright law.

Copyright © (Laurie F. Kimberly), (2024).

Disclaimer

The information contained in this book is for general informational purposes only. While we strive to provide accurate and up-to-date information, we make no representations or warranties of any kind, express or implied, about the completeness, accuracy, reliability, suitability, or availability with respect to the content contained within these pages for any purpose.

The information is provided by the author(s) and contributors and while we endeavor to keep the information up to date and correct, we make no representations or warranties of any kind, express or implied, about the completeness, accuracy, reliability, suitability, or availability with respect to the book or the information, products, services, or related graphics contained in the book for any purpose.

Any reliance you place on such information is therefore strictly at your own risk. In no event will we be liable for any loss or damage including without limitation, indirect or consequential loss or damage, or any loss or damage whatsoever arising from loss of data or profits arising out of, or in connection with, the use of this book.

Acknowledgments

I'm significantly appreciative of every individual who has added to the formation of "**unleashing your potentials: a journey to personal mastery**." This book has been a beautiful source of both blessing and pain, and I'm lowered by the chance to impart my bits of knowledge and encounters to you.

I, first and foremost, would want to offer my most profound thanks to the spearheading writers whose work in the field of self-awareness has significantly affected my life and roused me to compose this book. Extraordinary thanks to Tony Robbins, whose immortal insight on self-improvement and strengthening has filled in as a directing light on my excursion.I will likewise want to stretch out my genuine appreciation to my family for their unfaltering adoration, backing, and support all through the creative cycle. To my mate, whose confidence in my capacities never faltered, and whose unending persistence and understanding made it workable for me to seek after my enthusiasm for composing. To my kids, whose endless excitement and interest help me to remember the significance of embracing life's excursion with bliss and miracle. At long last, I need to offer my thanks to you, the peruser, for leaving on this excursion of individual dominance with me. It is my earnest expectation that the bits of knowledge and systems partook in this book will engage you to release your maximum capacity and make the existence of your fantasies.

About the Author

Laurie F. Kimberly is a dedicated self-help coach, mentor, and motivational speaker who is passionate about empowering individuals to unlock their full potential and live their best lives. With a background in psychology and personal development, Laurie has spent over a decade helping people break through barriers, overcome challenges, and achieve their goals.

Driven by a deep commitment to personal growth and transformation, Laurie has dedicated herself to helping others cultivate the mindset, skills, and habits necessary for success and fulfillment

Her relentless pursuit of excellence and her unwavering belief in the transformative power of personal development have inspired and motivated countless individuals to embark on their own journey of self-discovery and empowerment.

Her work as a coach and mentor, Laurie is also an avid writer and speaker. Through her books, articles, and public appearances, she seeks to reach a broader audience and spread her message of hope, empowerment, and possibility to all who are ready to embrace change and create a life they love.

Laurie holds a Bachelor's degree in Psychology and is certified in various modalities of personal development and coaching. When she's not coaching clients or writing, Laurie enjoys spending time in nature, practicing yoga, and exploring new ways to nurture her mind, body, and spirit.

INTRODUCTION	**8**
Chapter 1	**13**
Setting the Foundation	13
Chapter 2	**23**
Crafting Your Strategy	23
Chapter 3	**37**
Taking Massive Action	37
Chapter 4	**49**
Navigating Challenges	49
Chapter 5	**60**
Tracking Progress	60
Chapter 6	**74**
Maximizing Productivity	74
Chapter 7	**87**
Harnessing Motivation	87
Chapter 8	**101**
Effective Communication	101
Chapter 9	**115**
Embracing Accountability	115
Chapter 10	**129**
Celebrating Success	129
Conclusion	**143**

INTRODUCTION

Imagine waking up one morning feeling lost and unfulfilled, wondering if there's more to life than the daily grind. You drag yourself out of bed, trudge through your routine, and go through the motions, all the while feeling a sense of emptiness gnawing at your soul. This was me not too long ago—a mere shadow of the person I knew I could be, trapped in a cycle of mediocrity and dissatisfaction.

But one day, everything changed. It wasn't a sudden epiphany or a miraculous stroke of luck. It was a steady arousing — an acknowledgment that I held the way to opening my maximum capacity and making the existence I really wanted. Thus started my excursion to individual dominance — an excursion of self-disclosure, development, and change that would perpetually modify the direction of my life.

In "Unleash Your Potential: A Journey to Personal Mastery," I welcome you to leave on a comparative excursion — an excursion of strengthening and edification that will enable you to break liberated from the chains of self-uncertainty and restriction and step into your significance. Through a blend of viable methodologies, helpful stories, and extraordinary activities, this book will direct you on a way of self-disclosure and self-improvement, engaging you to release your maximum capacity and make the existence of your fantasies.

Growing up, I was dependably a visionary — a youngster with enormous desires and, surprisingly, greater yearnings. However, as I aged, life appeared to work on my fantasies, leaving me feeling disappointed and crushed. I made due with a task that covered the bills however didn't satisfy me, and I started to surrender to an existence of calm franticness.

It was only after I wound up in a very difficult situation that I understood something needed to change. I was fed up with only existing — I needed to live genuinely. Thus, I settled on a choice — a choice to assume command over my predetermination and seek after my interests with enduring assurance. It was difficult, and there were numerous snags en route, yet with each challenge came a chance for development and self-disclosure.

Through long stretches of experimentation, I found the force of individual dominance — the capacity to saddle my internal assets and make the existence I wanted. I discovered that genuine satisfaction comes not from outer accomplishments or honors but rather from a profound feeling of direction and arrangement with my qualities and yearnings. What's more, above all, I discovered that the way to opening my possible lay inside me from the start — I simply required the boldness to trust in myself and make a move.

And now, I want to share what I've learned with you. In "Unleash Your Potential," you'll find useful methodologies for laying out and accomplishing your objectives, developing a development mentality, defeating self-restricting convictions, and developing strength notwithstanding misfortune. You'll figure out how to take advantage of your inward assets and gifts, influence the force of positive reasoning and perception, and make a guide for progress that lines up with your most profound cravings and desires.

However, this book is something beyond an assortment of procedures and strategies — it's a guide for change. Every part is intended to rouse and enable you to make a move and step into your significance. From characterizing your vision and explaining your objectives to defeating delaying and constructing strong organizations, "Unleash Your Potential" provides you with the tools and insights you need to create the life you desire and deserve.So assuming that you're prepared to break liberated from the chains of self-uncertainty and restriction, in the event that you're prepared to step into your power and release your maximum capacity, then, at that point, I welcome you to go along with me on this excursion of individual dominance. Together, we'll set out on a way of self-revelation, development, and change that will enable you to carry on with an existence of energy, reason, and satisfaction. Is it safe to say that you are prepared to release your true capacity?

Chapter 1

Setting the Foundation

Defining Your Vision

Your vision is the underpinning for setting out on any critical journey toward individual or mastery development. It fills in as the coordinating light, the North Star, which facilitates your exercises and decisions generally throughout the journey toward your goals. Your vision epitomizes your most significant longings, desires, and values, delineating the future you attempt to make. At its essence, portraying your vision incorporates digging deeply into your most profound considerations and feelings to uncover the primary thing to you. It requires reflection and care to recognize your inclinations, resources, and core values. Track down a valuable chance to ponder your life's inspiration, considering questions like, for instance, What gives me delight and fulfillment? What legacy might I want to forsake? What impact do I look to make on the world?

Your vision should be striking and trying, stretching out past the restrictions of your continuous circumstances. It should move you and convince you to push past your standard scope of commonality and seek after importance. Imagine the future you need with clarity and distinction, imagining everything about it as if it were, by then, a reality. Imagine the outcomes you wish to achieve as well as the singular you try to all the while. Nevertheless, describing your vision isn't simply training to live in a dreamland. It requires sound judgment and legitimacy to ensure that your cravings are achievable and in accordance with your abilities and resources. Consider your resources, capacities, and areas for improvement as you make your vision, characterizing forceful yet plausible goals that push you toward progress. Also, your vision should be versatile and flexible, fit for progressing as you progress on your outing. Embrace change and embrace weakness, seeing that unforeseen hardships and astounding entryways could arise in transit. Remain liberal and receptive to extra open doors, changing your vision depending upon the situation to stay predictable with your general explanation and values. Finally, portraying your vision is a significantly private and drawn-in connection that clears a path for momentous turns of events and fulfillment. It empowers you to get a sense of ownership over your destiny, coordinating your exercises with reason and deliberateness. Embrace the power of your vision, and let it go about as the primary impulse behind your excursion to achieve your targets and manifest your dreams. Portraying Your Vision is a course of soul-looking and reflection that goes beyond a basic goal-setting process. It's connected to exploiting your most significant desires and desires, allowing them to coordinate you far ahead. This insightful outing requires dependability with yourself, preparation to challenge your sensations of fear, and the strength to think past functional limits. As you leave on the trip to describe your vision, quieting the upheaval of outside suspicions and social tensions is huge. Taking everything into account, direct your attention inside and pay concentration to the mumbles of your heart. What influences your energy? What gives your life importance and inspiration? By reconnecting with your most profound desires, you can uncover a fantasy that resonates significantly with who you are. Your vision should be an impression of your characteristics, convictions, and necessities. It should represent the epitome of what your personality is and be a major inspiration for you. Cut out the chance to research the most compelling thing about you—past shallow desires or passing longings. Consider the legacy you want to forsake and the impact you want to have on your overall environmental factors. In portraying your vision, it's important to think long, stretch, and contemplate the end-all strategy. While transient targets are critical for progress and energy, your vision fills in as the coordinating star that illuminates your direction toward a delightful future. It's the target toward which all of your exercises and decisions are arranged, giving clarity and bearing amid weakness. Regardless, portraying your vision is not a one-time event but rather a ceaseless course of refinement and improvement. As you create and progress, so too will your vision. Embrace the journey of self-revelation and give yourself the valuable chance to dream, explore, and rename what accomplishment means for you. Moreover, your vision should be hopeful yet achievable, broadening you beyond your standard scope of commonality while still inside the space of likelihood. Separate your vision into additional, unassuming, massive advances that you can require consistently to push closer toward your goals. Acclaim your headway on the way and stay zeroed in on the vision that fills your energy and reason. Portraying your vision is connected to changing your exercises to reflect your most significant characteristics and desires. It's connected to living truly and intentionally, with clarity and reason. Embrace the power of your vision, and permit it to stir you to make the presence you care about.

Clarifying Your Goals

While your vision gives the general course, your goals go about as significant accomplishments in transit. They are the construction blocks that change your vision from a distant dream into a significant reality. To make sense of your targets really, starting by changing them to your vision is urgent. Your targets should be the same, with the general explanation and values outlined in your vision. Track down a chance to consider how each goal adds to the affirmation of your vision; it is critical and purposeful to ensure that they do. Whenever you've spread out the game plan between your targets and vision, the result is to make them splendid: unequivocal, quantifiable, attainable, huge, and time-bound. Expressivity is key in portraying unequivocally the specific thing you want to achieve, precluding obscurity or irregularity. Quantifiability grants you the right to watch your turn of events and applaud your victories in transit. Possibility ensures that your goals are reachable, yet at this point, they are moving with the eventual result of expanding your capacities. Significance ensures that your targets are huge and agree with your vision and values. At last, time-boundness gives you a need to hurry up and an obligation, rousing you to take action and focus on your targets. While making sense of your targets, considering both present second and long-term goals is moreover critical. Fleeting goals give you the speedy moves you need to make to make strides, while long-strength targets offer a greater perspective on where you should be from now on. By balancing transient triumphs with long-stretched desires, you can stay aware of the power and remain prodded all through your journey. Plus, it's important to zero in on your targets given their importance and impact. Not all goals are the same, and some could have a more unmistakable significance in attracting you closer to your vision. Perceive the serious-need targets that will generally influence your trip and spotlight your critical interest in achieving them first. As you make sense of your targets, try to stay versatile and flexible. Life is overflowing with surprising, energizing curves in the street, and your targets ought to be changed in transit. Embrace change as a trademark piece of the connection and turn when it is essential to stay in agreement with your vision. Making sense of your goals is compared to making a clear aid that guides you on your journey toward your vision. As an aide gives clear direction and places of interest to show up at your goal, making sense of your targets spreads out the accomplishments and markers that mean progression and achievement. One of the most essential parts of making sense of your targets is ensuring that they are deeply rooted in your characteristics and desires. Your goals shouldn't simply reflect what you want to achieve but, moreover, why it means a lot to you as an individual or at a significant level. By partnering your goals with your most significant desires and motivations, you instill them with reason and significance, making them genuinely persuading and moving. Likewise, making sense of your goals incorporates isolating them into reasonable and critical stages. Rather than setting muddled or overwhelming targets, attempt to portray exercises and accomplishments that attract you closer to your goals. This course of obliterating your objectives into extra humble parts makes them more conceivable as well as provides a manual for advancement and commitment. One more piece of figuring out your objectives is guaranteeing that they are concurred with your assets, limits, and assets. Consider what you win at and what assets are available to you, and affect them to portray objectives that exploit your innate limits and lift your possibilities, ending up as the best. This strategy helps your conviction as well as builds your ability to chase after your objectives. Additionally, it's vital to fan out assessments and pointers to monitor your improvement toward your objectives. By depicting clear degrees of progress, you can screen your show, perceive regions for development, and recognize your accomplishments on the way. These assessments go about as guideposts that keep you associated with and persuaded, guaranteeing that you stay on track toward your vision. As well as portraying focus on huge results, taking into account objectives that focus on self-improvement and improvement is moreover squeezing. These objectives could consolidate getting new limits, vanquishing restricting convictions or making positive affinities that help your excursion towards your vision. By setting resources into your self-awareness, you update your capacities as well as cultivate your strategy with your vision. Getting a handle on your objectives requires a stance of flexibility and strength. See that difficulties and inconveniences are certain in transit to accomplishing your targets, and be prepared to adjust your direction depending upon the situation. Embrace disillusionments as learning open entryways and use them to refine your procedure and support your motivation. Essentially, making sense of your targets is a multifaceted interaction that incorporates partnering them to your characteristics, isolating them into critical stages, changing them to your resources and resources, spreading out estimations for following headway, developing personal growth, and staying aware of solidarity regardless of trouble. By zeroing in on your goals with clearness and deliberateness, you set yourself in a decent situation on your trip toward your vision.

Chapter 2

Crafting Your Strategy

Creating a Winning Plan

Making a victorious game plan is the platform that interfaces your vision and targets to critical stages and undeniable results. The chart changes your desires into this present reality, giving the fundamental framework and course expected to investigate the complexities of achieving your goals. The most crucial stage in making a victorious plan is to coordinate a cautious assessment of your continuous situation and resources. This incorporates looking at your resources, deficiencies, open entryways, and risks (SWOT examination), as well as perceiving any goals or limitations that could influence your ability to achieve your targets. By securing an unquestionable appreciation of your early phase, you can utilize your resources and ease your inadequacies to support your chances of ending up as the winner. Whenever you have overviewed your continuous situation, the accompanying stage is to describe your objectives and results. What expressed results might you want to achieve? What accomplishments will test your headway in transit? By setting clear and quantifiable targets, you make an aide that coordinates your exercises and decisions generally through the execution of your plan. With your objectives set up, the resulting stage is to recognize the frameworks and techniques expected to achieve them. This incorporates isolating your goals into additional humble and huge stages and choosing the best approaches for accomplishing each one. Ponder what resources, capacities, and gadgets will be supposed to execute your course of action successfully, and dole out them fittingly. Plus, making a victorious game plan requires a wary idea of schedules and deadlines. Spreading out sensible schedules for every time of your game plan helps with making a need to hurry up and obligation, ensuring that you stay on track and make predictable progress towards your targets. Know about logical obstacles or delays that could arise in transit and work on substitute blueprints to ease their impact. As well as representing the specific exercises expected to achieve your goals, a victorious game plan should further integrate frameworks for checking and surveying progress. This incorporates spreading out key execution pointers (KPIs) and accomplishments to monitor your turn of events, as well as reliably examining and considering your show in contrast to these benchmarks. By staying wary and proactive in noticing your progress, you can separate districts for advancement and roll out crucial improvements as per your game plan. Besides, making a victorious plan incorporates developing a mindset of adaptability and strength. See that amazing troubles or changes could arise during the execution of your plan, and be prepared to turn and change your procedure depending upon the situation. Keep a responsive viewpoint and remain versatile in your thinking, embracing change as an opportunity for improvement and headway. Building an Aide for Success Creating a victorious plan isn't just about portraying a movement of endeavors; about making a fundamental design that increases your chances of beating the competition. It requires a wary idea of various components, from your resources and resources for the external environment to anticipated tangles. By embracing a comprehensive procedure for organizing, you can set yourself up in a decent way and investigate the complexities of achieving your targets with sureness. One of the basic parts of making a victorious plan is ensuring a game plan between your objectives and your overall vision. Your course of action shouldn't exist in isolation anyway and should be associated with the greater explanation and heading outlined in your vision. This game plan gives a sensation of sufficiency and motivation to your exercises, ensuring that each step you treat contributes remarkably to the affirmation of your excessively long targets. Plus, making a victorious plan incorporates characterizing limits and making fundamental tradeoffs. Not all targets and objectives are of identical importance, and you could need to arrive at problematic decisions about where to administer your time, energy, and resources. By focusing on high-impact activities and drives that change personally with your vision and targets, you can grow your practicality and achieve further development in less time. Besides, a victorious game plan requires clearness and expression in outlining the exercises and steps expected to achieve your objectives. Avoid dark or ambiguous language, and things being what they are, provide clear rules and guidance for execution. Separate your course of action into additional unobtrusive, sensible endeavors, and spread out liability instruments to ensure that progress is being made and deadlines are being met. Besides, making a victorious game plan incorporates using your resources to their fullest potential. Recognize the capacities, gifts, and assets that you have and consider how you can include them for your likely advantage in seeking after your targets. Know about any openings or areas where additional assistance or resources may be required, and search for opportunities to fill those openings through joint exertion, reexamining, or capacity headway. As well as outlining the exercises expected to achieve your objectives, a victorious game plan should similarly consolidate plausibility measures for overseeing frightening hardships or incidents. Expect potential obstructions or risks that could arise during the execution of your course of action, and cultivate strategies for lightening their impact. By preparing for the unexpected, you can restrict aggravations and focus on pushing forward towards your targets. At long last, making a victorious game plan requires nonstop noticing and evaluation to follow progress and measure accomplishment. Regularly review your game plan against spread-out estimations and accomplishments, and change your philosophy relying upon the circumstance, considering analysis and results. Compliment your victories on the way, yet moreover gain from disillusionments and disasters to continually refine and chip away at your plan after some time. Making a victorious game plan is like making a masterpiece—a meticulously organized troupe of exercises, methodology, and resources expected to push you toward your targets with exactness and reason. It's connected to envisioning the future you need and illustrating a system that changes that vision into this present reality. In its middle, making a victorious game plan requires a significant cognizance of your objectives and the factors that influence their satisfaction. This includes coordinating a thorough examination of your inside and external environment, perceiving open entryways for improvement, and being true to the risks and impediments that could upset your headway. By getting clarity on these factors, you can cultivate procedures that impact your resources and reduce your deficiencies, arranging yourself for results despite trouble. Plus, making a victorious game plan incorporates characterizing clever targets—express, quantifiable, practical, critical, and time-bound—that give clear heading and fixation. These goals go about as the accomplishments that mark your progression and guide your exercises, ensuring that each step you take brings you closer to your last area. By isolating your goals into sensible tasks and spreading out deadlines for getting done, you make a need to get rolling and an obligation that drives energy and keeps you on track. Besides, a victorious game plan requires a fundamental viewpoint that embraces versatility and adaptability. While it's crucial to have an undeniable aide for achieving your goals, remaining open to new entryways and surprising upgrades in transit is likewise huge. Turn and change your game plan depending upon the situation, making the most of possibilities and acquiring from frustrations to refine your technique and stay agreed with your vision. As well as outlining the specific exercises expected to achieve your objectives, a victorious game plan should similarly ponder the human part: your gathering, accomplices, and empowered gathering. Energize open correspondence and collaboration, connecting with your associates to contribute their clever perspectives and capacities to the total effort. Foster a culture of trust, obligation, and shared ownership, where everyone is changed around a common explanation and zeroes in on gaining ground together. Moreover, making a victorious plan incorporates looking at and assessing progress against laid benchmarks and KPIs (Key Execution Pointers). Reliably assess your show, recognize locales for advancement, and celebrate wins in transit. By monitoring your advancement continuously, you can recognize examples, models, and encounters that enlighten the route and drive relentless improvement. Making a victorious game plan isn't just about achieving transient results; it's also about developing long-term legitimacy and strength. Ponder the greater consequences of your exercises and decisions, and attempt to make regard that loosens up past brief outcomes. Collect associations, associations, and structures that help your targets and add to your long advancement, ensuring that your undertakings yield getting through impact and huge change. By and large, making a victorious game plan is a comprehensive and iterative cycle that requires key thinking, clarity of heading, composed exertion, adaptability, and an energetic commitment to significance. By pushing toward organizing with deliberateness and foresight, you can change your desires into achievements and chart a course toward a destiny of boundless possibility and potential.

Building a roadmap

Building an aide for progress is similar to illustrating a course for a journey; it gives the bearing, accomplishments, and strategies expected to investigate the way towards your targets with clearness and sureness. about making a fundamental design that coordinates your exercises and decisions, ensuring that each step you take attracts you closer to your optimal goal. In its middle, creating an aide for progress begins with a sensible understanding of your objectives and the outcomes you wish to achieve. Track down an open door to make sense of your targets and objectives, both present second and long stretch, and describe the specific results you want to accomplish. Your aide should change personally with these objectives, outlining the exercises and approaches expected to convey them to the end. Plus, fabricating an aide for progress incorporates isolating your goals into additional unassuming, vital advances that are reachable and quantifiable. Think about these methods' accomplishments along your trip, indicating your headway and assigning assigned spots for evaluation and appraisal. By isolating your goals into sensible endeavors, you gain a sensation of energy and headway that keeps you enlivened and focused. Besides, building an aide for progress requires a wary idea of the resources, capacities, and gadgets expected to execute your plan effectively. Recognize the assets and capacities you have, as well as any openings or locales where additional assistance may be required. Consider how you can utilize your resources and alleviate your deficiencies to support your chances of beating the competition. As well as outlining the specific exercises expected to achieve your targets, your aide should similarly consider potential obstructions and troubles that could arise on the way. Expect likely risks and encourage crisis approaches to address them, ensuring that you are prepared to investigate startling circumstances with adaptability and adaptation. Moreover, building aid for progress incorporates characterizing limits and making crucial trade-offs. Not all targets and objectives are of identical importance, and you could need to arrive at problematic decisions about where to administer your time, energy, and resources. By focusing on high-impact activities and drives that change personally with your vision and targets, you can grow your practicality and achieve further development in less time. Besides, building aid for progress requires ceaseless noticing and evaluation to follow the progress and measure accomplishment. Regularly review your game plan against spread-out estimations and accomplishments, and change your philosophy relying upon the circumstance, considering analysis and results. Praise your victories on the way, yet also gain from dissatisfactions and accidents to continually refine and deal with your course of action after some time. By and large, constructing an aide for progress is a dynamic and iterative cycle that requires key thinking, clarity of course, virtuosity, adaptability, and an industrious commitment to significance. By pushing toward organizing with deliberateness and foresight, you can change your desires into achievements and chart a course toward a destiny of boundless possibility and potential. Building an aide is similar to making an organized manual that edifies the way toward your goals with clearness and exactness. It incorporates twisting around various parts, from your vision and focus to methodology and resources, into a solid plan that fills in as a graph for progress. The key to building an aide is the course of essential thinking and orchestrating. This includes envisioning the best outcomes and portraying the means expected to achieve them. It requires a complete understanding of the greater scene—both inside and outside factors—that could influence your trip, allowing you to expect challenges and potential entryways in transit. Moreover, building an aide incorporates changing your objectives to your general vision and values. Your aide shouldn't exist in restriction anyway and should be connected with the explanation and heading delineated in your vision. By laying out your plan from a more significant point of view of bearing, you gain a sense of clarity and a game plan that coordinates your exercises with intentionality and importance. Moreover, building an aid requires isolating your goals into huge advances that make a sensible pathway forward. This incorporates portraying unequivocal endeavors, accomplishments, and courses of occasions that frame your progression and give a sense of direction. By breaking your goals into additional unobtrusive, sensible parts, you make an aide that is both suitable and reachable, empowering a sensation of energy and progress. As well as delineating the specific exercises expected to achieve your goals, creating an aide incorporates contemplating the resources, capacities, and instruments expected for execution. This could integrate assessing your resources and capacities, recognizing likely openings or areas for advancement, and scanning out significant entryways for composed exertion or mastery improvement. By using your resources, truth be told, you can intensify your chances of dominating the competition and vanquish any hindrances that could arise in transit. Furthermore, building an aide requires constant checking and evaluation to follow progress and measure accomplishment. This incorporates spreading out key execution pointers (KPIs) and accomplishments that go about as benchmarks for examination. By regularly looking over your presentation against these estimations, you can recognize areas for improvement, roll out essential improvements, and commend your achievements on the way. Building an aide is a dynamic and iterative collaboration that requires key thinking, a game plan with your vision and values, rational goal setting, virtuosity, and predictable checking and evaluation. By pushing toward organizing with deliberateness and feeling, you can make an aide that coordinates your journey toward progress with clarity, reason, and flexibility.

Chapter 3

Taking Massive Action

Overcoming Procrastination

Beating waiting is a common test that numerous people could seem, by all accounts, to be harmless. Persevering delay can have serious results, provoking missed deadlines, extended pressure, and diminished productivity. At its middle, faltering much of the time begins from a blend of mental, near and dear, and social factors. The sensation of fear toward disillusionment, hairsplitting, shortfall of motivation, and inconvenience managing time are two or three of the essential issues that can add to slowing down. Understanding these essential causes is major to beating waiting and recuperating orders throughout your time and effectiveness. One of the most amazing strategies for overcoming waiting is to recognize and address the hidden drivers of your wavering. Track down an open door to ponder why you will frequently waver. Is it probably true that you dread frustration or examination? Do you fight with hair-splitting or self-questioning? By procuring information about the fundamental purposes for your tarrying, you can cultivate frameworks to determine these issues and break free from the example of postponing. Moreover, vanquishing waiting requires creating care. Center around your perspectives, opinions, and approaches to acting when you end up delaying. Notice any models or triggers that add to your dawdling, and challenge negative thought models or self-limiting convictions that may be holding you down. By becoming more aware of your dawdling inclinations, you can begin to track down proactive ways of changing them. Another suitable framework for vanquishing tarrying is to isolate endeavors into additional unassuming, more sensible advances. Oftentimes, postponing arises out of feeling overwhelmed or unsure where to start. By isolating endeavors into additional humble, essential stages, you can make them feel more reasonable and less overpowering. Set unequivocal, attainable targets for each step of the task, and focus on completing them carefully. This helps with diminishing impressions of overwhelm as well as gives pride and progress in transit. In addition, laying out a coordinated environment can help decrease the likelihood of waiting. Set up a committed workspace that is freed from interferences and supportive for fixation and concentration. Spread out a regular practice or schedule for taking care of tasks, and stick to it whatever amount as could sensibly be anticipated. Put down clear places to pause around your huge venture, and shine on tasks considering their importance and centrality. By laying out a coordinated environment, you can restrict interferences and set aside a supportive room for proficiency. Likewise, crushing delay requires creating self-control and building sound inclinations. Set forth unambiguous targets and deadlines for yourself, and see yourself as liable for social occasions. Break tasks into additional unobtrusive, sensible protuberances, and set aside dedicated time consistently to manage them. Practice balance and resolve by contradicting the motivation to delay and staying fixed on your goals. Also, searching for help from others can be instrumental in vanquishing deferring. Share your targets and troubles with associates, family, or accomplices who can extend encouragement, obligation, and sponsorship. Consider working with a guide or expert who has a common involvement with productivity and utilizing time successfully to encourage modified methods for overcoming hesitating. By enlisting the assistance of others, you can secure critical pieces of information and motivation to help you stay centered. Vanquishing dillydallying isn't just about finding helpful arrangement game plans or using unyielding time-use methodology; it's connected to fostering a mindset shift and embracing viable penchants that advance productivity and success. It requires a widely inclusive system that watches out for the secret explanations behind delaying while similarly developing adaptability and self-control. One essential piece of vanquishing slowing down is encouraging an improvement standpoint—a conviction that your abilities and information can be improved through effort and steadiness. By embracing an improvement mindset, you can reexamine challenges as entryways for advancement and learning instead of obstacles to be avoided. This demeanor shift draws in you to advance toward tasks with interest and fervor rather than fear or repugnance. Likewise, beating yourself down incorporates reexamining your relationship with dissatisfaction. Various good-for-nothings are nitpickers who fear frustration and examination, driving them to slow down for fear of not satisfying their own high rules. By embracing disillusionment as a trademark and undeniable piece of the instructive experience, you can reduce the sensation of fear toward dissatisfaction and add your energy to confront difficulties and endeavor new things. View hardships as learning open entryways rather than evidence of your inadequacy, and use them to enlighten your turn of events and improvement. Another huge piece of waiting is building care. Center around the contemplations, opinions, and approaches to acting that trigger waiting, and cultivate procedures to manage them effectively. Practice care procedures like significant breathing, examination, or moderate muscle loosening to stay present and focused on the primary work. By creating care and caring, you can disrupt the example of dallying and make extra intentional choices about how you use your critical speculation. In addition, slowing down requires characterizing common goals and presumptions for yourself. Do whatever it takes not to spread out exorbitantly forceful or ludicrous goals that set you up for disillusionment and disappointment. Taking everything into account, separate greater targets into additional unobtrusive, more reasonable advances, and recognize your progression in transit. By defining feasible goals and recognizing your accomplishments, you build assurance and motivation to push ahead. Moreover, building a reassuring gathering can be instrumental in overcoming failure. Encompass yourself with sidekicks, family, or accomplices who engage in and maintain your undertakings to overcome faltering. Share your goals and troubles with them, and solicit their help and obligations when required. By selecting the assistance of others, you create a sense of obligation and motivation that can help keep you on track.

Cultivating Daily Habits for Success

Creating everyday affinities for progress is connected to spreading out timetables and practices that help your targets and objectives, inciting more noticeable productivity, fulfillment, and thriving. These inclinations go about as the foundation whereupon you can create a presence of course and achievement, coordinating your exercises and decisions toward progress for an anticipated reason. At the center of creating everyday affinities for progress is the affirmation that little, consistent exercises lead to enormous results after some time. By zeroing in on standard penchants and timetables, you make a development that enables you to make strides toward your targets consistently, paying little regard to outside conditions or interferences. These penchants become permeated into your standard daily practice, shaping your attitude and leading in habits that line up with your vision for progress. One imperative piece of creating regular penchants for progress is spreading out a morning plan that lays out the energy for the day ahead. A morning plan licenses you to start your day with deliberateness and reason, giving a sensation of plan and focus that brings you through to the rest of your day. This routine could consolidate practices like reflection, workouts, journaling, or objective setting, depending upon your tendencies and requirements. By starting your day, hopefully, you set yourself in a decent position and increase productivity throughout the day. Additionally, creating ordinary inclinations for progress remembers centering on tasks and activities that line up with your targets and values. Recognize the principal tasks or assignments that will attract you closer to your objectives and spotlight them in your everyday arrangements. Use gadgets, for instance, plans for the afternoon, timetables, or time-frustrating techniques to organize your tasks and apportion time for high-impact workouts. By focusing your massive speculation on endeavors that have the greatest effect, you enhance your proficiency and progress toward your targets. Another huge piece in creating ordinary penchants for progress is practicing patience and consistency. Accomplishment isn't achieved for now, yet it is the delayed consequence of little, unsurprising exercises reiterated over an extended time. Center around showing up reliably and contributing energy, regardless of when motivation is low or obstructions arise. By fostering a viewpoint of discipline and persistence, you build up strength and momentum that pushes you forward on your journey to advance. Additionally, creating regular penchants for progress incorporates empowering an improvement mindset—a conviction that your abilities and understanding can be improved through effort and practice. Embrace troubles as any entryway for improvement and learning, and push toward disasters as significant delineations that add to your new development. Foster a peculiarity and preparation to dominate new capacities and perspectives, and quest out open entryways for self-improvement and mindfulness. By embracing an improvement mindset, you let loose yourself to extra open doors and open your greatest limit concerning advancement. Besides, creating regular inclinations for progress requires managing your physical and mental health. Center around practices like action, suitable sustenance, adequate rest, and stress on the board to help your overall prosperity and noteworthiness. Put away a couple of moments for practices that give you joy and loosen up, whether it's financial planning energy with loved ones, pursuing side interests, or practicing care. By supporting your flourishing, you increase your adaptability and capacity to manage challenges, allowing you to perform at your best and gain ground in all parts of your life. Creating everyday penchants for progress is a journey of endless turn of events and improvement—an assurance to supporting affinities and timetables that connect with you to prosper in all pieces of your life. It's connected to embracing that accomplishment isn't just about achieving expressed goals or accomplishments anyway; it's about living with assumption and reason reliably. One crucial piece of creating everyday penchants for progress is laying out an environment that maintains your targets and objectives. Enclose yourself with people who move and convince you, and kill interferences or unfavorable effects that ruin your headway. Plan your genuine space to reflect your characteristics and necessities, making a workspace that supports focus and imaginativeness. By coordinating your ongoing situation to agree with your goals, you gain a foundation for headway that engages advancement and achievement. Moreover, creating everyday penchants for progress incorporates encouraging solid personality care and reflection. Take time consistently to evaluate your progression and study what's working commendably and what could be improved to a higher level. Journaling thoughts or mind practices can help you tune into your perspectives and feelings, allowing you to gain encounters with your affinities and approaches to acting. By creating care, you can perceive districts for advancement and carry out purposeful enhancements to help you flourish. Another critical piece of creating regular inclinations for progress is characterizing cutoff points and managing your time. Sort out some way to communicate no to activities or obligations that don't agree with your goals or values, and spotlight on tasks that add to your long advancement. Use instruments like timetables, coordinators, or proficiency applications to organize your plan and assign time for high-need workouts. By characterizing cutoff points and managing your time deliberately, you account for focused work and critical headway toward your goals. Additionally, creating everyday penchants for progress incorporates empowering strength and adaptability despite challenges and hardships. Understand that failure is a trademark piece of the instructive experience and an opportunity for advancement and improvement. Cultivate techniques for adjusting to strain and burden, for instance, practicing appreciation, searching for help from others, or partaking in dealing with one's activities. By creating flexibility, you manufacture the solidarity to get back from mishaps and continue to push ahead toward your goals. Moreover, creating everyday inclinations for progress requires a guarantee for well-established learning and personal development. Stay curious and liberal, looking for possible opportunities to develop your knowledge and capacities in areas relevant to your targets. Put assets into your tutoring and master development, whether through appropriate courses, studios, or free learning. By fostering an improvement viewpoint and embracing endless learning, you position yourself for progress in a consistently affecting world.

Chapter 4

Navigating Challenges

Overcoming Obstacles

Vanquishing obstructions is a characteristic piece of the journey toward progress. Whether they are external hardships, for instance, money-related necessities, or inside obstacles like self-vulnerability and fear, deterrents might conceivably wreck progress and obstruct achievement. Regardless, vanquishing blocks isn't simply possible yet in that frame of mind for advancement and adaptability. One basic piece of overcoming obstacles is encouraging a viewpoint of adaptability and affirmation. Rather than survey checks being troublesome obstacles, believe them to be open entryways for improvement and learning. Embrace incites as any open doors to test your endpoints, cultivate new capacities, and create adaptability despite the difficulty. By taking on an inspirational perspective and rethinking blocks as any entryway, you can push toward them with conviction and confirmation, understanding that you can beat them. Likewise, beating obstacles as often as possible requires inventive, decisive reasoning, and cunning. Instead of getting stopped by disasters, conceptualize elective game plans and ways of managing to make the test reachable. Kick-off something new and consider how you can utilize your resources, resources, and empowering gathering to find a way forward. By being flexible and versatile in your system, you can as often as possible track down imaginative responses for even the most overpowering tangles. Another critical piece of vanquishing obstacles is staying aware of fixation and energy despite trouble. It's easy to get prevented or fail to zero in on your targets when going up against challenges, yet it's important to stay committed and keep on pushing ahead. Separate the obstacle into additional humble, sensible advances, and focus on making continuous progress consistently. Celebrate little wins in transit to remain convinced and aware of power toward your goals. Also, beating impediments oftentimes involves searching for help from others. Make it a highlight to demand help or direction from buddies, family, guides, or accomplices who have defied practically identical troubles. Their pieces of information and perspectives can provide critical guidance and relief, helping you to investigate impediments even more. Moreover, enclosing yourself with a solid neighborhood takes confidence in your actual limit and urges you to persevere despite trouble. Additionally, beating obstacles incorporates managing your physical and mental well-being. Stress, exhaustion, and burnout can feel the impact of obstacles and make them harder to get by. Center around dealing with self-activities like movement, loosening up, and care to recharge your energy and flexibility. Practice self-compassion and thought toward yourself, seeing that appreciating respites and spotlighting your flourishing during testing times is alright. Beating hindrances requires an intricate philosophy that keeps an eye on both external hardships and inward limits. It's adequate not to simply have an uplifting perspective or rely solely upon decisive abilities to reason; taking everything into account, it's connected to uniting various frameworks and methods to investigate catches, as a matter of fact, and emerge more grounded on the contrary side. One dire piece of overcoming obstacles is having the capacity to see the value in people on a more profound level and with more care. This incorporates seeing and getting a handle on your sentiments, examinations, and reactions to testing conditions. By creating care, you can recognize any terrible models or limited convictions that may be adding to the obstacle and cultivate philosophies to supervise them all the more effectively. Besides, the ability to see the value in people on a more profound level licenses you to figure out others and investigate social battles or challenges, with no perspiration or style. Likewise, overcoming obstacles regularly requires adaptability—the ability to get back to challenges and burdens. Strength isn't connected to avoiding disillusionment or hardship but about acquiring from them and including them as any entryways for improvement. Foster strength by reconsidering troubles as any open doors for development, focusing on what you have some command over, and searching for help from others when required. By building adaptability, you can confront the difficulties of presence easily and emerge more grounded than beforehand. Another huge piece of vanquishing hindrances is making decisive abilities to reason and adaptability. When faced with a test, push toward it with a curious and responsive standpoint, researching substitute perspectives and anticipated plans. Investigate, face difficulties, and gain from disillusionments on the way. Also, be versatile and flexible in your system, seeing that the method for advancing is only sometimes straight and may require changes on the way. By using decisive reasoning skills and adaptability, you can investigate impediments even more effectively and find successful fixes to even the most troublesome issues. Also, beating impediments now and again incorporates spreading out clear goals and limits to coordinate your exercises and decisions. Perceive the fundamental targets or results you want to achieve, and focus your energy and resources around them. Slow down goals into additional unassuming, critical stages, and make an aide or plan to help you stay centered. By spreading out clear targets and limits, you can stay aware of focus and power, in any event, despite obstacles or interferences. Also, beating checks requires practicing dealing with oneself and zeroing in on one's flourishing. Cut out an open door to recharge your energy and flexibility through practices like movement, consideration, or concentrating intensely on nature. Center around strong affinities like getting adequate rest, eating nutritious food assortments, and regulating pressure. By managing your physical and mental thriving, you can extend your capacity to manage troubles and investigate with no perspiration and ease. Essentially, crushing impediments is a different cycle that requires the ability to grasp individuals on a significant level, adaptability, decisive abilities to reason, flexibility, objective setting, and dealing with oneself. By organizing these frameworks into your procedure, you can investigate obstacles even more effectively and emerge more grounded, more intelligent, and more prepared to achieve your targets and figure out your fullest potential.

Staying Resilient in the Face of Adversity

Staying adaptable despite trouble is connected to remaining strong, flexible, and certain, even in the most troublesome circumstances. It's connected to returning rapidly from accidents, finding strength in mishaps, and continuing to push ahead notwithstanding hindrances. The following are a couple of focal issues to consider concerning areas of strength for staying: Embrace the Power of Perspective: Foster a positive mindset that believes challenges are open entryways for improvement and learning. Rethink incidents as temporary deterrents instead of unimaginable limits. Revolve around what you have some command over and let go of what you can't change. Gather the ability to figure out individuals at their center: Encourage care to see and manage your sentiments. Practice caring systems to remain grounded and present even with trouble. Foster compassion and sympathy for yourself as well as other people, understanding that everyone faces fights. Support a Consistent Association: Encompass yourself with associates, family, and guides who offer reassurance and sponsorship. Search out genuine models who have crushed similar hardships and draw inspiration from their records. Make it a highlight to demand help when required, and lay on your reassuring gathering for safety and comfort. Foster Strength Through Dealing with Oneself: Center around dealing with oneself activities like action, reflection, and side interests that give you delight and loosen up. Appreciate respites when expected and focus on your body's finished paperwork for rest and recovery. Put down places to pause to protect your critical speculation, communicating no to activities or obligations that channel you. Practice flexibility and adaptability: Change your game plans and procedures due to advancing circumstances. Look for insightful fixes and elective ways when faced with hindrances. Recall that hardships are not dissatisfactions but instead, opportunities to course right and endeavor again. Revolve around characteristics and resources: Perceive your resources, capacities, and resources that can help you with investigating trouble. Draw on past experiences of solidarity and achievement to recall your capacities. Search out important opportunities to utilize your resources and resources for vanquished hindrances. Keep an Internal Compass and significance: Connect with

Unleashing your potentials

your characteristics and long-term stretch targets to remain convinced and focused during irksome times. Find importance in trouble by looking for open entryways for mindfulness and obligation to others. Remember that challenges are brief, but your ability to know east from west and adaptability can continue. Staying flexible regardless of hardship isn't just an issue of rapidly getting back from setbacks; it's connected to thriving amid troubles and emerging more grounded and more capable on the opposite side. It requires a significant vault of internal strength, flexibility, and brightness that licenses you to investigate life's ups and downs with style and adaptability. One part of staying flexible is embracing the power of disposition. Your mindset shapes how you interpret and answer trouble, influencing whether you believe blocks to be negative preventions or entryways for advancement. Foster an advancement viewpoint that viewpoints incite as any entryways to learn and improve, rather than fixed requirements on your actual limit. By taking on a good and flexible mindset, you can push toward incidents with a sensation of certainty and confirmation that empowers

57

you to overcome even the hardest challenges. Furthermore, staying flexible notwithstanding disaster remembers fabricating the capacity to see the value in individuals for a more profound level of care. The ability to see the value in people on a more profound level licenses you to see and handle your sentiments as well as the sensations of others, which is huge for investigating predicaments with compassion and class. Practice care systems like significant breathing, reflection, or journaling to remain grounded and present at that point, regardless, while defying trouble. By creating the capacity to see the value in anybody at their center and care, you can answer troubles with more noticeable clarity, understanding, and flexibility. Besides, staying solid even with mishaps requires supporting a consistent association of friends, family, and mentors who can extend encouragement, bearing, and perspective during inconvenient times. Circle yourself with people who put confidence in your ability to beat hardships and who stir you to push ahead, regardless of whatever inconveniences emerge. Search out genuine models who have stood up to difficulty with adaptability and ease, and draw inspiration from their records of wins and energy. By developing serious areas of fortitude for an association, you make a security net of relief and endorsement that upholds your adaptability even with trouble. Also, staying solid even with torment centers on dealing with oneself and flourishing. Carve out a time to help your physical, mental, and up-close and personal prosperity through practices like action, great counting calories, good rest, and stressing the load-up systems. Put down places to pause to shield your huge venture, and spotlight on practices that give you delight, loosening up, and fulfillment.

Chapter 5

Tracking Progress

Implementing Effective Metrics

Completing strong estimations is key for following headway, assessing execution, and driving advancement in any endeavor. Estimations give huge pieces of information into key areas of execution, helping affiliations and individuals seek informed decisions, perceive districts for advancement, and achieve their targets. Here are start-to-finish pieces of information for completing practical estimations: Clarity of Heading: Before executing estimations, it's essential to have an indisputable understanding of the explanation and objectives you want to achieve. Describe your goals and needed results with precision, ensuring they are unequivocal, quantifiable, reachable, appropriate, and time-bound (smart). This clearness of heading will coordinate the assurance of fitting estimations and assurance course of action with comprehensive key targets. Key Game plan: Estimations should be immovably agreed with the fundamental necessities and focuses of your affiliation or undertaking. Ensure that each estimation directly adds to the satisfaction of greater goals and supports the overall mission and vision. By changing estimations to imperative objectives, you make a strong design for assessing accomplishment and driving progression in the best bearing. Importance and Reality: Pick estimations that are significant to your specific layout and objectives. Avoid the impulse to follow estimations basically because they are easy to check or speedily open. Taking everything into account, based on estimations of huge encounters and critical signs of progress toward your goals, ponder both proactive variables (sightful of future execution) and coincidental outcomes (smart of past execution) to procure a careful point of view on progress. Quality Data Variety and Assessment: Assurance of the precision, steady quality, and authenticity of data accumulated for estimations via completing solid data grouping and assessment processes Use standardized methods and contraptions for data arrangement and spread out clear shows for data on the board and quality affirmation. Put assets into advancement and assessment capacities to streamline data collection, examination, and specification, enabling lucky and exact heading. Tenacious Checking and Evaluation: Complete a structure for steady checking and appraisal of estimations to follow progress, perceive floats, and review execution for a long time. Reliably review and inspect metric data to recognize emerging issues, perceive areas for advancement, and benefit from open entryways. Use data discernment methodologies like dashboards, scorecards, and reports to give disclosures, as a matter of fact, and work with a data-driven heading. Benchmarking and Assessment: Use benchmarking and connections with contextualized metric data and look at execution near industry standards, best practices, or competitors. Perceive benchmarks and key execution markers (KPIs) that are pertinent to your one-of-a-kind circumstance and use them as reference centers for setting targets and surveying execution. Benchmarking gives significant pieces of information into strong regions and inadequacy, including important entryways for improvement and headway. Analysis and Change: Develop a culture of steady improvement by mentioning analysis from accomplices and incorporating pieces of information procured from metric data into dynamic cycles. Use estimations as a gadget for learning and change, rather than as a static extent of execution. Stimulate open talk and joint exertion among partners to recognize likely entryways for development and improvement considering metric encounters. Straightforwardness and Obligation: Assurance of straightforwardness and obligation in the use of estimations by conveying targets, suppositions, and execution results clearly and straightforwardly Spread out parts for liability to ensure that individuals and gatherings are viewed as obligated to achieve targets and fulfill execution rules. Develop a culture of straightforwardness, where metric data is expeditiously open to accomplices and used to drive liability and improvement. Executing feasible estimations isn't just about following numbers or assembling data; it's connected to driving huge change and achieving needed results. To jump further into this point, could we research additional encounters and strategies for using estimations to drive accomplishment: Game plan with Various Leveled Characteristics and Culture: Estimations shouldn't exist in isolation yet should be significantly organized into the definitive characteristics and culture? Ensure that the estimations you choose to follow reflect the core values, needs, and long-term vision of your affiliation. Change estimations to social norms and suppositions, empowering buy-in and obligation from all accomplices. By embedding estimations inside the progressive surface, you make a typical language and understanding of execution that develops needed approaches to acting and results. Versatility and Adaptability: While it's fundamental to spread out clear estimations and execution centers around, remaining versatile and flexible due to changing circumstances is comparably basic to propel needs. See that estimations are still hanging out there anyway and may be changed or refined long term considering new information, analysis, or changes in technique. Be accessible to getting back to and refreshing estimations relying upon the circumstance, ensuring they stay significant, huge, and agreed with various leveled targets. Compromise Across Capacities and Divisions: Fruitful estimations execution requires joint exertion and coordination across various abilities and workplaces inside an affiliation. Separate storage facilities and support a cross-helpful plan by spreading out shared goals and estimations that cut across definitive cutoff points. Stimulate joint exertion and correspondence among gatherings to ensure a widely inclusive method for managing execution assessment and improvement. By organizing estimations across abilities, you make agreeable energies and intensify the impact of execution drives. Highlight on Proactive Variables and Perceptive Examination: While following outcomes give significant pieces of information into past execution, proactive elements offer farsighted encounters into future outcomes. Put a more unmistakable compliment on proactive elements that can help with recognizing early notification signs, anticipating designs, and proactively addressing potential issues before they arise. Impact judicious examination and show strategies to figure out future execution considering undeniable data and examples. By focusing on proactive elements and farsighted assessment, you can arrange your relationship for progress and stay ready. Steady Learning and Improvement: View estimation execution as a consistent trip of learning and improvement, rather than a one-time workout. Support a culture of steady learning and experimentation, where frustrations are viewed as entryways for improvement and headway. Develop a sensation of premium and solicitation, engaging individuals and gatherings to research novel contemplations, test speculations, and challenge assumptions. By embracing a mindset of determined improvement, you create a dynamic and flexible affiliation that twists despite weakness and change. Moral Considerations and Social Commitment: While executing estimations, ponder the ethical repercussions and social commitment of your exercises. Ensure that the estimations you track line up with moral rules and norms, and that they don't unexpectedly help destructive or exploitative approaches to acting. Think about the greater social and environmental impacts of your affiliation's activities, and attempt to balance money-related execution with social commitment. By coordinating moral examinations into estimation execution, you can develop trust, acceptability, and liberality with accomplices and society at large. Noticing Accomplishments and Seeing Achievements: Finally, make sure to celebrate accomplishments and see achievements on the way. Perceive and compensate individuals and gatherings who meet or outperform execution targets, and laud accomplishments and achievements all around. Lauding accomplishment develops profound fulfillment, motivation, and fraternity among partners, developing sure approaches to acting and results. By lauding accomplishment, you create a culture of appreciation and affirmation that is continued with execution and accomplishment.

Adjusting and Course-Correcting

Altering and direction curing are principal parts of any outing toward progress. Notwithstanding how particularly organized or executed a system may be, there may be unexpected troubles and developing circumstances, and it is certain to shock. At such critical points in time, to change, change, and course right becomes vital to staying centered and achieving needed results. One of the essential norms of altering and direction curing is keeping a standpoint of versatility and adaptability. As opposed to unyieldingly adhering to a destined game plan, turn and make changes relying upon the circumstance, considering new information, analysis, or creating conditions. Embrace weakness as a characteristic piece of the outing and advance toward hardships with interest, straightforwardness, and adaptability. By fostering a versatile attitude, you can answer effectively to changing conditions and investigate obstructions with ease and conviction. Another critical piece of altering and direction-helping is regularly taking a look at progress and execution to perceive locales for improvement or refinement. Spread out clear estimations and execution pointers to follow progress toward goals, and regularly review and examine data to study execution and recognize designs. Be proactive in searching for analysis from accomplices and mentioning input from associates to secure various perspectives and encounters. By staying cautious and proactive in noticing execution, you can recognize early exhortation signs and address issues before they escalate. Also, altering direction during an excitement to surrender bungles and gain from dissatisfactions Instead of viewing adversities as confirmation of frustration or inadequacy, believe them to be open entryways for improvement and learning. Embrace an improvement mindset that values experimentation, cycles, and relentless improvement. Think about past experiences, the two triumphs and disillusionments, to isolate significant models and encounters that enlighten future decisions and exercises. By embracing dissatisfaction as a trademark and essential piece of the developing experience, you can change hardships into wandering stones toward progress. Additionally, shifting and direction correction incorporate using information and data to enlighten free bearing and guide exercises. Use data-driven encounters and verification-based examination to recognize areas of underperformance or disappointment and spotlight locales for advancement. Be proactive in searching for analysis from accomplices, clients, and partners to obtain significant encounters with their necessities, tendencies, and suspicions. By incorporating analysis and data into dynamic cycles, you can make extra taught and fundamental choices that lead to further-developed results. Likewise, altering and direction correcting require feasible correspondence and joint exertion among associates and accomplices. Develop open trade and straightforwardness, engaging partners to share contemplations, concerns, and thoughts for advancement. Make a culture of trust and mental security where individuals feel empowered to holler and cause trouble. Group up cross-basically to utilize various perspectives and fitness, and remember accomplices for the unique cycle to ensure plan and buy-in. By developing correspondence and collaboration, you can handle the total information and creative mind of your gathering to drive reasonable shifts and direction corrections. Shifting and direction changing are fundamental pieces of any powerful trip, whether in business, mindfulness, or another endeavor. It's basic to see that no course of action spreads out exactly true to form, and unanticipated challenges or astonishing entryways could arise in transit. Thus, the ability to change and roll out fundamental improvements is basic for staying centered and, in the long run, achieving the needed results. One piece of shifting and direction modification incorporates keeping a proactive situation toward change. Rather than believing that issues will arise or conditions will be met to coordinate a response, screen progress and anticipate likely obstructions or deviations from the plan. By staying ready and being proactive in perceiving locales for transformation, you can restrict the impact of aggravations and stay aware of energy toward your goals. Plus, shifting and direction correction require status to challenge assumptions and embrace weakness. See that even the most carefully made plans rely upon assumptions that may not be guaranteed to turn out true to form. Be accessible to examining these assumptions and reconsidering your strategy, considering new information or advancing circumstances. By embracing weakness as a trademark piece of the outing, you can change even more expeditiously to amazing energizing twists in the street, changing troubles into significant entryways for improvement and headway. Another critical piece of shifting and direction curing is keeping an improvement standpoint. As opposed to studying disasters or deviations from the plan as dissatisfactions, believe them to be astonishing entryways for learning and improvement. Embrace a mindset of interest and experimentation, scanning out new strategies and dealing with any consequences regarding road impediments. By reexamining mishaps as open doors for development, you can isolate significant pieces of information that enlighten future decisions and exercises, finally inciting more critical strength and accomplishment. Moreover, altering and direction redressing incorporate fruitful bearing and prioritization. When faced with different decisions or methodologies, mindfully survey the normal risks and grants of every other choice, weighing transient increases against long-stretch targets. Center around switches that line up with crucial goals and have the best potential for impact, instead of simply answering the most speedy hardships. By chasing after the lessons and key decisions, you can direct the course toward progress in any event, despite weakness. Besides, shifting and direction revision of suitable correspondence and facilitating exertion across all levels of affiliation or gathering make channels for open talk and information, enabling individuals to share pieces of information, concerns, and thoughts for advancement. Support a culture of straightforwardness and obligation where everyone feels empowered to add to the change cycle. By outfitting the total knowledge and creative mind of your gathering, you can perceive innovative game plans and execute changes even more as a matter of fact.

Chapter 6

Maximizing Productivity

Time Management Techniques

Time utilization methodology is central for helping productivity, restricting strain, and achieving a sensation of balance and fulfillment in both master and individual lives. Strongly utilizing time isn't just about being involved or affirming tasks; it's connected to zeroing on what has the greatest effect, upgrading work processes, and seeking deliberate choices about how to administer the venture. We ought to research start-to-finish encounters and strategies for ruling utilizing time really: One basic rule of feasible utilizing time is prioritization. Rather than endeavoring to deal with every task on your arrangement for the afternoon, revolves around recognizing and zeroing in on tasks that line up with your goals, values, and necessities. Use systems, for instance, the Eisenhower Network or the ABCD strategy to orchestrate tasks considering importance and distress, and appropriate your time and resources similarly. By focusing on serious need tasks first, you can ensure that you are making progress on the primary thing most and do whatever it takes not to get slowed down by less huge or minor activities. Another key piece of utilizing time beneficially is spreading out clear targets and objectives. Describe your long targets and separate them into additional unobtrusive, huge stages or accomplishments. Set deadlines and courses of occasions for getting done with tasks and exercises, and use instruments like timetables, coordinators, or undertaking the chief's applications to screen deadlines and obligations. By having an indisputable aid for what you want to achieve and when, you can remain focused and convinced, using your time and resources. What's more, convincingly utilizing time beneficially incorporates further developing work interaction and taking out time-wasting activities or interferences. Perceive typical time drains, for instance, preposterous social occasions, email over-weight, or performing different errands, and execute approaches to restrict or discard them. Use techniques, for instance, time ruining or bunching near endeavors together to help efficiency and breakpoint setting trading. Put down places to pause around your time and sort out some way to communicate no to activities or obligations that don't agree with your targets or needs. By streamlining your work interaction and diminishing interferences, you can save an open door for high-regard practices and achieve more unmistakable effectiveness and fixation. Besides, utilizing time successfully requires discretion and care. Be clear with yourself about your resources, weaknesses, and penchants concerning managing your time. Recognize instances of waiting or time screw-ups and encourage methods to overcome them. Practice patience by characterizing clear cutoff points around your time and sticking to them, regardless of when defied by allurements or interferences. Use systems, for instance, the Pomodoro Technique or the 2-minute rule to break tasks into additional unobtrusive, reasonable pieces and stay aware of energy. By creating restraint and care, you can overcome ordinary time-use hardships and use your critical speculation. Besides, convincing yourself to utilize time successfully incorporates managing your physical and mental flourishing. Center around practices like movement, loosening up, and dealing with oneself that recharge your energy and adaptability. Get adequate rest, eat nutritious food assortments, and supervise pressure to ensure that you are working at your best. Focus on your body's signs, appreciate respites when expected to remain offset, and stay aware of productivity. By zeroing in on your thriving, you can work on your presentation and benefit from your time and resources. Ruling and utilizing time gainfully is a well-established adventure that requires constant reflection, refinement, and change. As you try to propel your use of time and resources, think about researching additional strategies and frameworks to redesign your sufficiency and effectiveness. One area to explore is bunching equivalent endeavors together to augment adequacy and cutoff-setting trading. As opposed to jumping between immaterial tasks throughout the day, gather relative activities and tackle them in focused blocks of time. For example, dole out unequivocal timetable openings for noting messages, making phone choices, or managing creative undertakings. By clustering tasks together, you can restrict interferences and impedances, allowing you to work even more capably and stay aware of revolving around the primary work. Another technique to consider is time obstructing, which incorporates arranging committed blocks of time for express activities or endeavors. Administer time on your timetable for critical tasks, social occasions, and plans, and treat these blocks of time as hallowed liabilities to yourself. Avoid overcommitting or arranging back-to-back get-togethers, and be intentional about defending your huge speculation. Via completing time prevention, you can make a coordinated framework for managing your day and ensure that you have committed energy for both significant need tasks and individual activities. Moreover, consider examining the principles of significant work and focused care regarding enhancing your proficiency and creativity. Significant work remembers lowering yourself for a task or adventure with full obsession and consistent fixation, allowing you to achieve a state of stream and produce incredible work. Center around significant work gatherings during times when you feel prepared and stimulated, and lay out a good environment free from interference. By embracing significant work guidelines, you can open your greatest limit and produce huge results faster than anticipated. In addition, don't dismiss the meaning of tasks by reexamining them in a way that utilizes time beneficially. See that you can't do everything yourself, and delegate tasks to others who are more able to manage them. Perceive areas of your obligation that could be assigned to partners, associates, or reconsidering assistants, and draw them in to accept ownership and responsibility. By naming endeavors effectively, you can save extra money by opening the door for high-regard practices that line up with your resources and requirements. What's more, consider using development and robotization gadgets to streamline dull tasks and add capability. Research programming applications, effectiveness applications, and undertaking the chiefs' contraptions that can help you automate routine cycles, track progress, and manage your obligation even more in fact. From time following and undertaking the load up to email robotization and arranging instruments, there are different development plans open to help you improve your time and work process. Attempt various things with different gadgets and methodologies to find what ends up being brutal for you and direct them into your ordinary everyday timetable.

Boosting Efficiency and Focus

Helping capability and focus are keys to achieving maximum activity and growing productivity in both master and individual endeavors. By stepping up your ability to work even more really and staying aware of the spotlight on critical tasks, you can accomplish surprisingly quickly and achieve more conspicuous satisfaction and fulfillment. Could we research a start-to-finish encounter and philosophies for overhauling capability and fixation? One fundamental norm for supporting viability and focus is spreading out unequivocal goals. Portray what you want to accomplish and isolate your targets into additional unassuming, sensible tasks or accomplishments. By spreading out clear objectives, you can keep a sense of direction and reason, simplifying it to zero in on endeavors and staying fixed on what has the greatest effect. Moreover, set deadlines and schedules for finishing liabilities to make a need to continue moving and energy, driving you to take action and make progress toward your targets. Another crucial piece in aiding adequacy and focus is restricting interferences and impedances. Perceive typical wellsprings of interference like email, electronic amusement, or loud circumstances, and do frameworks to restrict their impact on your work interaction. Use methodology, for instance, time deterring or characterizing limits around your reality, to make dedicated periods for focused work. Contemplate using instruments or applications that block redirecting locales or cutoffs during seasons of concentrated focus. By laying out a supportive environment for centers, you can restrict interference and stay aware of your thoughts on huge endeavors. Additionally, helping efficiency and focus incorporates propelling your work interaction and streamlining cycles to restrict pointless scouring or wasted effort. Recognize the district of your work interaction that could be automated, appointed, or improved to augment adequacy and diminish mental weight. Look for astonishing opportunities to take on or join low-regard tasks and smooth out grim cycles. By smoothing out your work interaction, you can save extra time and mental information by limiting high-regard practices that require focus and inventiveness. Besides, it fosters affinities and timetables that help uphold fixation and productivity. Spread out a typical plan or everyday timetable that consolidates committed time for focused work, breaks, and seasons of rest and recovery. Center around practices like movement, reflection, or care practices that advance mental clearness and adaptability. Make customs or prompts that signal the start of focused work gatherings, for instance, turning off sees, putting on external surrounding noise-canceling headphones, or lighting a fire. By laying out a supportive environment and spreading out consistent inclinations, you can set up your brain to enter a state of stream even more successfully and stay aware of your obsession with testing tasks. Besides, supporting viability and focus incorporates managing your energy levels and keeping a sound harmony among fun and serious exercises. See that your energy is a restricted resource that ought to be recharged reliably through rest, loosening up, and dealing with oneself. Focus on your body's signs, appreciate respites when expected to remain offset, and stay aware of expanded execution. Center around practices past work that give you delight, fulfillment, and importance, such as money management energy with loved ones, seeking relaxation exercises, or participating in creative pursuits. By supporting your physical, mental, and significant thriving, you can uphold raised levels of focus and proficiency long term. Supporting capability and focus isn't just about using unambiguous strategies or techniques; it's about fostering a mindset and lifestyle centering around productivity, reasonability, and thriving. To dive further into this point, could we research additional pieces of information and perspectives for overhauling viability and focus? One critical piece supporting efficiency and focus is the possibility of proactive energy for the leaders. Instead of essentially managing your time, base it on managing your energy levels throughout the day. See that your energy wavers over an extended time, with standard apexes and valleys, and plan your activities in like manner. Plan high-energy tasks that require phenomenal fixation during your active times, and save low-energy periods for extra everyday timetable or less mentioning works. By changing your tasks according to your energy levels, you can enhance proficiency and stay aware of upheld focus throughout the day. Furthermore, helping capabilities and focus incorporate fostering an advancement mindset that embraces challenges and values learning and improvement. As opposed to viewing hardships or obstructions as disillusionments, believe them to be open entryways for advancement and improvement. Embrace a mindset of consistent learning and experimentation, looking for new experiences and challenges that stretch your abilities and broaden your perspectives. By taking on an improvement mindset, you can push toward tasks with more important strength, creativity, and confirmation, inciting updated capability and fixation. Likewise, consider the occupation of the environment and ecological variables as affecting capability and fixation. Make a workspace that is useful for obsession and effectiveness, with insignificant interferences and wrecks. Put assets into ergonomic goods, authentic lighting, and disturbance-dropping headphones to lay out a pleasing and interference-free environment. Enclose yourself with enticing prompts like awakening articulations, pictures, or articles that assist you in recollecting your goals and wants. By working in your genuine environment, you can create the best conditions for empowering capability and focus. Also, helping efficiency and focus incorporates making frameworks for supervising information over-weight and decision shortcomings. In the current high-velocity world, we are bombarded with a stunning proportion of information and choices every day, which can provoke mental fatigue and decreased productivity. Do techniques like Information Crisis, where you quickly assess the importance and significance of moving toward information and spotlight it as required. Limit the number of decisions you want to make through robotizing routine endeavors or spreading out clear, unique measures. By lessening mental weight and decision shortcomings, you can set free mental exchange speed for more critical and valuable work. What's more, think about the meaning of attitude and disposition in supporting efficiency and fixation. Foster a rousing point of view toward your work and hardships, considering them to be any entryways for advancement and achievement instead of loads or checks. Practice appreciation and mind to foster a sensation of presence and fixation at that point, allowing you to attract with your tasks and commitments. Encourage an ability to know east from west and the importance of your work, communicating your ordinary activities with greater goals and values that energize and prod you. By embracing a positive mindset and disposition, you can redesign your flexibility, imaginativeness, and focus, provoking more essential efficiency and accomplishmen.

Chapter 7

Harnessing Motivation

Cultivating a Growth Mindset

Fostering an improvement viewpoint is an unprecedented trip that empowers individuals to embrace troubles, gain from dissatisfactions, and deliver their most extreme limit. Grounded in the conviction that limits and information can be made through responsibility and troublesome work, an improvement viewpoint develops adaptability, relentlessness, and a love for learning. We ought to explore this thought from start to finish and reveal essential pieces of information for fostering an improvement standpoint: At the center of an improvement standpoint is the conviction that capacity and information are not fixed qualities, but rather qualities that can be created and made after some time. As opposed to survey achievement as the outcome of inherent limits, individuals with an improvement viewpoint believe it to be the consequence of effort, steadiness, and acquiring from messes up. This adjustment of setting opens up a vast expanse of possible results, empowering individuals to push toward hardships with positive reasoning and confirmation. They are still hanging out there, knowing that their abilities are there. Plus, fostering an improvement mindset incorporates reevaluating disasters and frustrations as an entryway for advancement and learning. Rather than survey dissatisfaction as confirmation of deficiency or insufficiency, individuals with an improvement standpoint consider it to be a trademark piece of the developing experience. They embrace dissatisfaction as a critical wellspring of information and grasping, allowing them to perceive districts for improvement and refine their technique. By reexamining troubles thusly, individuals can become rapidly more grounded, changing obstacles into wandering stones toward progress. Besides, fostering an improvement viewpoint requires empowering friendship for learning and interest on Earth. Instead of studying progress as an errand or responsibility, individuals with an improvement viewpoint approach it with energy and excitement, believing every understanding to be an opportunity to expand their knowledge and capacities. They search out new hardships and experiences, impelling themselves past their standard scopes of commonality and embracing the pain that goes with improvement. By fostering a fondness for learning, individuals can open their most extreme limits and achieve astounding results in both their own and capable lives. Besides, fostering an improvement mindset incorporates encouraging a sensation of coarseness and confirmation notwithstanding trouble. Instead of giving up when faced with impediments or incidents, individuals with an improvement viewpoint progress forward in pursuing their goals, in any event, despite hardships or disasters. They view obstructions as short-lived blockades that can be overpowered with effort and industriousness, instead of amazing limits. By creating coarseness and affirmation, individuals can investigate even the most problematic circumstances with flexibility and ease, emerging more grounded and more equipped than at some other time. Furthermore, fostering an improvement viewpoint incorporates encompassing oneself with consistent individuals and conditions that energize advancement and improvement. Search our guides, tutors, and companions who energize and incite you to extend past your limits and have a go at significance. Enclose yourself with positive effects and genuine models who typify the attributes and values you attempt to foster in yourself. Lay out conditions, both physical and social, that help risk-taking, experimentation, and advancement. By circling yourself with resilient individuals and conditions, you can create a ready ground for fostering an improvement mindset and achieving your fullest potential. Fostering an improvement standpoint isn't just about embracing another conviction structure; it's about, from an overall perspective, changing how we approach challenges, disasters, and important entryways for improvement. To jump further into this subject, we ought to explore additional encounters and frameworks for fostering an improvement mindset: One point to consider is the meaning of reevaluating blunders and dissatisfactions as significant learning experiences. Rather than study frustration as an impression of individual worth or limits, individuals with an improvement standpoint consider it to be a trademark piece of the instructive experience. They see that each mistake is an opportunity to gain understanding, refine their philosophy, and at last grow further and more grounded. By reconsidering messes up thusly, individuals can overcome the misgiving about dissatisfaction and embrace hardships with assurance and certainty. Furthermore, fostering an improvement standpoint incorporates cultivating character, care, and self-reflection. Track down a potential open door to contemplate your convictions, points of view, and approaches to acting, and consider what they mean for your ability to learn and create. Recognize any appropriate attitudes or limiting convictions that may be holding you down, and challenge them with verification and sensible thinking. Foster a standpoint of straightforwardness and interest, remaining open to analysis and ready to change your perspective when thinking about new information. By taking care and self-reflection, you can break free from mental blocks and open your greatest limit concerning advancement and improvement. Besides, think about the job of flexibility and assurance in fostering an improvement mindset. See that turn of events and progress are not commonly straight, and setbacks and hindrances are inevitable en route to advance. Foster adaptability by using strategies for real-life adaptations and significant rule techniques to investigate troubles with magnificence and flexibility. Embrace the power of resoluteness by zeroing in on your goals and wants in any event, despite the burden. By creating adaptability and assurance, individuals can confront the difficulties of presence with strength and emerge more grounded than at any time in ongoing memory. Moreover, fostering an improvement standpoint incorporates developing a sense of obligation regarding one's learning and improvement. Rather than relying upon external components or conditions to coordinate their thriving, individuals with an advancement mindset track down proactive ways of expecting control over their turn of events and improvement. Set forth clear goals and focuses for yourself, and view yourself as liable for making progress toward them. Scan out important entryways for improvement and headway, whether through appropriate preparation, mentorship, or free learning. By getting a sense of ownership of your learning and improvement, you can foster a sensation of association and reinforcement that stimulates your turn in events and accomplishment. Furthermore, consider the meaning of flexibility-building exercises like appreciation, care, and self-compassion in fostering an improvement mindset. Foster appreciation for the entryways, experiences, and troubles that add to your turn of events and improvement. Practice care to foster care and presence at that point, allowing you to attract your experiences and gain from them. Cultivate self-compassion by treating yourself with liberality and sorting it out, especially amidst inconvenience or dissatisfaction. By coordinating these adaptability consolidating practices into your everyday day-to-day practice, you can foster a standpoint of adaptability and advancement that empowers you to vanquish any obstacle and achieve your fullest potential.

Finding Inspiration and Drive

Finding inspiration and drive is key to gaining ground and fulfillment in both individual and master endeavors. It fills our energy, lights our creative minds, and drives us forward, pursuing our goals and dreams. Could we research this subject all around and reveal essential encounters for finding inspiration and drive? One fundamental piece of finding inspiration and drive is fostering an internal compass and importance in our lives. Cut out an open door to contemplate your characteristics, interests, and wants, and consider how they line up with your greater goals and targets. Perceive activities, causes, or errands that resound significantly with you and bring a sensation of fulfillment and satisfaction. By interacting with your internal compass, you can exploit a significant source of motivation and drive that controls your exercises and prompts you toward your targets. Likewise, finding inspiration and drive incorporates looking through the wellsprings of inspiration and motivation that influence you before long. Circle yourself with people, books, craftsmanship, music, or experiences that awaken and hoist you, filling you with energy and fervor until the end of time. Search for mentors, genuine models, or sidekicks who exemplify the attributes and values you try to foster in yourself and gain from their knowledge and experiences. By lowering yourself into conditions and organizations that empower inspiration and drive, you can fuel your excitement and motivation to achieve importance. Besides, finding inspiration and drive requires keeping an improvement mindset and a sensation of interest in and marveling about the world. Push toward each day with a responsive viewpoint and an enthusiasm to explore novel considerations, experiences, and entryways. Embrace hardships as any entryways for improvement and learning, instead of obstacles to be avoided. Foster a sensation of interest in your overall environmental elements by getting explanations of major problems, looking through new perspectives, and attracting various social orders and considerations. By embracing a standpoint of premium and examination, you can uncover new wellsprings of inspiration and drive that fuel your capable turn of events. Additionally, finding inspiration and drive incorporates spreading out forceful yet reachable goals that stretch your abilities and push you past your standard scope of commonality. Describe unequivocal targets that line up with your characteristics and objectives, and separate them into additional humble, essential stages or accomplishments. Set deadlines and schedules for completing tasks and endeavors, making a need to get rolling and energy that drives you forward. By advancing critical targets and taking anticipated action toward achieving them, you can exploit areas of strength for inspiration and drive that push you toward progress. Plus, finding inspiration and drive incorporates fostering a positive and flexible viewpoint that enables you to vanquish obstacles and incidents on the way. See that hardships and adversities are undeniable and headed toward advance, but they don't describe your worth or potential. Foster strength by reevaluating incidents as entryways for advancement and learning and by making strategies for practical adaptations and significant rule techniques to investigate inconvenient times with ease and adaptability. By fostering a positive and flexible standpoint, you can stay aware of your motivation and drive in any event, despite mishaps, and emerge more grounded and more skilled than at any time in late memory. Finding inspiration and drive is a significantly confidential journey that requires examination, care, and status to embrace change and improvement. As we investigate the complexities of life, it's generally expected to encounter seasons of stagnation, vulnerability, or weakness. Regardless, by successfully looking through our wellsprings of inspiration and supporting our internal drive, we can reignite our energy, imaginativeness, and motivation to seek after our dreams with restored power and confirmation. One in-number strategy for finding inspiration and drive is by lowering ourselves in nature and the greatness of our overall environmental elements. Nature has a way of dealing with stirring our resources, laying out us at present, and assisting us with recollecting the interconnectedness of every living thing. Whether it's living in the mountains, watching the nightfall by the ocean, or concentrating on a nearby park, being in nature can give a critical sensation of stunningness and wonder that stretches creative minds and inspiration. By connecting with the normal world, we can exploit a significant wellspring of inspiration and drive that controls our imaginative endeavors and invigorates our spirits. Furthermore, finding inspiration and drive incorporates scanning out astounding entryways for improvement and self-disclosure. Partake in practices that challenge you to step past your standard scope of commonality, whether it's dominating another skill, agreeing on a particular position interest, or pursuing a significant endeavor. Embrace the course of experimentation and examination, allowing yourself to commit blunders and gain from them in transit. By driving yourself to endeavor new things and develop your perspectives, you can track down hidden away capacities and endless interests that fuel your inspiration and drive. Besides, finding inspiration and drive requires fostering a sensation of appreciation for the blessings in our lives. Take time consistently to consider the things you are thankful for, whether it's the fondness for friends and family, the greatness of nature, or the entryways for improvement and finding that consistently brings. Foster a mindset of flood and appreciation, seeing that even amid troubles, there is a ton to be thankful for. By focusing on the positive pieces of life, we can foster a viewpoint of confidence and adaptability that empowers our inspiration and drive. Besides, finding inspiration and drive incorporates communicating with our interior explanation and interests. Cut out a valuable open door to consider the primary thing to you, what gets a fire moving in your soul, and what you feel called to pursue with energy and fervor. Perceive your essential convictions, interests, and desires, and change your exercises and goals to reflect these fundamental beliefs. By living within a game plan with your internal explanations and interests, you can exploit a significant stock of inspiration and drive that pushes you forward on your trip toward fulfillment and accomplishment. Furthermore, finding inspiration and drive requires empowering a sensation of neighborhood relationship with others who share our characteristics, goals, and wants. Encompass yourself with consistent and comparable individuals who lift and propel you, whether it's through joining a neighborhood gathering, going to Framework Organization events, or participating in online conversations and discussions. Participate in critical conversations and joint endeavors with others, sharing considerations, pieces of information, and experiences that ignite your energy and creative mind. By fostering consistent neighborhood colleagues and guides, you can draw strength, backing, and inspiration from the total understanding and energy of everybody around you.

Chapter 8

Effective Communication

Communicating Your Vision

Bestowing your vision is a fundamental piece of drive and accomplishment, as it incorporates moving and rejuvenating others around a typical point of view and bearing. Whether you're driving a gathering, starting another undertaking, or supporting an explanation, strong correspondence of your vision is central to changing accomplices, building up momentum, and driving progression toward your goals. We ought to explore this subject from start to finish and reveal important encounters for conveying your vision in fact: One basic piece of conveying your vision is clarity—having the choice to communicate your vision in an unquestionable, brief, and persuading way that resonates with your group. Cut out a valuable open door to distill your vision into a direct and basic message that gets the substance of what you're endeavoring to achieve. Use language that is accessible and connects with your group, avoiding language or particular terms that could remove or perplex your group. By examining your vision with clarity, you can ensure that everyone understands and shares your internal compass and bearing, developing a plan and fortitude. Moreover, granting your vision incorporates spreading out an unmistakable and propelling picture addressing what might be on the horizon—one that gets the imaginative brain and lights energy and fervor in others. Use describing systems to restore your vision, twisting around and putting together records, stories, and models that outline the impact and importance of your vision. Appeal to the sentiments and desires of your group, exploiting their assumptions, dreams, and desires for an unrivaled future. By making a persuading vision that reverberates on a significant level, you can move others to oblige you in conveying it to the end. Moreover, conveying your vision requires realness and straightforwardness—being genuine and authentic about your convictions, values, and motivations. Share your journey and experiences, including the troubles and blocks you've looked at along the way and how they have shaped your vision for what the future holds. Be accessible to analysis and commitment from others, inviting trade and facilitating exertion in pursuing shared targets. By displaying validity and straightforwardness, you can build trust and credibility with your group, developing a sensation of affiliation and shared respect. Moreover, conveying your vision remembers drawing for and empowering others to become dynamic individuals in figuring out that vision. Welcome data and responsibilities as indicated by grouped perspectives, seeing that turn of events and advance regularly emerge from participation and total effort. Set out open entryways for talk and the exchange of contemplations, engaging open correspondence, and significant information. Draw in others to get a sense of ownership of the vision and contribute their original gifts and capacities toward its affirmation. By developing a culture of composed exertion and reinforcement, you can handle the total energy and imaginativeness of your gathering or neighborhood and achieve astonishing results. What's more, conveying your vision requires consistency and emphasis—developing your message through various channels and touchpoints to promise it resonates with your group over an extended period. Use an arrangement of correspondence channels, similar to get-togethers, presentations, messages, and electronic amusement, to contact different groups and send key messages. Go over your vision reliably, fitting it into conversations, updates, and discussions to keep it on top of the cerebrum for every single closely involved individual. By staying aware of consistency and emphasis in your correspondence attempts, you can develop the importance and sincerity of your vision, main impetus, and progress toward your targets. Conveying your vision isn't just about sending information; it's connected to having a common viewpoint and internal compass that convinces and sets others up toward a common goal. To bounce further into this subject, could we research additional encounters and frameworks for truly conveying your vision? One critical piece of delivering your vision is accommodating your message to resound with your group. See that different accomplices could have fluctuating perspectives, interests, and needs, so it's fundamental to change your correspondence style and content to resolve their issues. Track down an open door to get a handle on your group's characteristics, concerns, and wants, and fashion your message properly. Use language and models that reverberate with their experiences and interests, making your vision significant and persuading them. By tweaking your correspondence with your group, you can grow responsibility and buy-in, developing a more significant awareness of others' expectations and commitment to your vision. Additionally, giving your vision incorporates using description as a basic resource for responsibility and impact. Make stories that show the outing and impact of your vision, twisting around together parts of feeling, battle, and objective to enchant your group's thought. Share records of individuals or affiliations who have been earnestly affected by your vision, including the significant benefits and results they have experienced. By framing your vision in the setting of persuading stories, you can make it fascinating and essential, bringing sympathy and awakening movement. Additionally, showing your vision requires full focus and trade to support two-way correspondence and participation. Set out open entryways for analysis and discussion, inviting requests, concerns, and considerations from your group. Listen carefully to their perspectives and pieces of information, displaying reverence and openness to alternate points of view. Participate in useful talks to address any off-track decisions or assurances from your vision, searching for a shared view and a normal point of view. By developing open correspondence and talk, you can build trust, empower facilitated exertion, and support game plans around your vision. Plus, bestowing your vision incorporates showing others how it's finished and embodying the characteristics and principles you embrace. Show realness, uprightness, and obligation in a way that would seem normal to you and exercise, changing your approach to acting to reflect the vision you hope to bestow. Model the approaches to acting and viewpoints you wish to track down in others, persuading them to follow you and embrace your vision as their own. By showing others how it's finished, you can stir endless trust in your power, empowering a culture of liability and a plan that pushes your vision forward. Furthermore, passing your vision requires flexibility and versatility to answer changing circumstances and analyze. Be accessible to refining and accentuating your vision, considering new information or pieces of information that emerge over a long time. Demand analysis and commitment from others, coordinating their perspectives and contemplations into your vision as fitting. Remain deft and responsive in your correspondence approach, changing your illumination and methods relying upon the circumstance to address creating challenges or astonishing entryways. By staying versatile and flexible, you can ensure that your vision stays relevant, persuasive, and critical, even with change.

Building Supportive Networks

Fabricating consistent associations is a groundwork for progress in both individual and master life. These associations outfit us with the sensation of being in a spot, offer huge resources and encounters, and go about as a wellspring of help and motivation during testing times. We ought to dive further into this point and examine systems for building and supporting consistent associations: One basic piece of building consistent associations is creating genuine relationships with others considering normal respect, trust, and correspondence. Rather than moving closer to the framework of an organization as a worth-based exchange of favors or contacts, it revolves around building certified associations in light of shared interests, values, and targets. Track down a valuable open door to get to know people on a singular level, showing confirmed interest in their lives, experiences, and objectives. Be open and direct about your targets and troubles, allowing others to interact with you on a more significant level. By growing genuine affiliations, you can manufacture solid areas for help and composed exertion that improves your life and work. Additionally, fabricating consistent associations incorporates looking through our grouped perspectives and experiences, which test and move us to create. Encompass yourself with individuals who bring different establishments, expertise, and viewpoints to the table, expanding your perspectives and pushing you past your standard scope of commonality. Partake in conversations and joint endeavors with people from different ventures, disciplines, and social establishments, embracing the luxury and assortment of human experience. By introducing yourself to various perspectives, you can secure new pieces of information, extend your understanding, and foster an additional thorough and thoughtful point of view. Additionally, constructing consistent associations requires being proactive and deliberate when scanning out open entryways for affiliation and participation. Go to frameworks organization events, social occasions, and studios associated with your tendencies and targets, where you can meet comparable individuals and possible colleagues. Join capable affiliations, neighborhood social affairs, or online conversations where you can attract others who share your inclinations and values. Take care of business and contact people you appreciate or respect, conveying your benefit to partners and acquiring from them. By being proactive in building your association, you can broaden your circle of help and open up new entryways for advancement and joint exertion.

Additionally, assembling consistent associations incorporates supporting and staying aware of associations for a long time through standard correspondence and responsibility. Stay in touch with your contacts through messages, calls, or virtual diversion, sharing updates on your progression, achievements, and challenges. Offer your endless help to others when they need it, whether it's through giving insight, making introductions, or offering a listening ear. Show appreciation for the responsibilities and support of your association people, seeing the value they bring to your life and work. By investing effort and effort in supporting your associations, you can foster serious solid areas for a solid association that upholds you through a wide range of difficulties. Furthermore, building solid associations incorporates being a liberal and consistent person from your neighborhood, your time, expertise, and resources to assist others with succeeding. Volunteer your time for purposes and affiliations that line up with your characteristics and interests, where you can make a huge difference and have a connection point with comparative individuals. Share your knowledge and capacities with others through coaching, training, or showing open entranceways, drawing in them to show up at their most extreme limit. Be a patron and accomplice for underrepresented social occasions or limited organizations, using your honor and effect to upgrade their voices and support their goals. By compensating your neighborhood and supporting others, you invigorate your association as well as add to everybody's advantage and make a more far-reaching major area of strength for and. Building solid associations isn't just about developing the amount of contacts in your area book—it's connected to creating significant, critical associations that work on your life and draw in you to achieve your targets. To jump further into this subject, could we examine additional pieces of information and approaches for building and supporting consistent associations? One essential piece of serious strength for the building is being proactive in scanning out astonishing entryways for affiliation and participation. Make an effort not to hold on to organizational events or chance encounters to expand your association. Move forward and search out significant opportunities to interact with others who share your tendencies and targets. This could incorporate reaching anticipated mentors, going to industry social events or meetups, or participating in online organizations and conversations. By tracking down proactive ways of building your association, you can broaden your circle of help and open up new entryways for composed exertion and improvement. Moreover, assembling consistent associations incorporates being key in the way you foster associations and contribute your critical speculation. As opposed to broadening yourself unreasonably far by endeavoring to keep endless shallow affiliations, based on building a more unobtrusive, even more intently sew association of trusted accomplices and partners, recognizing key individuals who can give critical encounters, resources, or sponsorship, and spotlighting supporting those associations, put time and effort into getting to know these individuals on a more significant level, and be purposeful about staying aware of standard correspondence and responsibility, By focusing in on better norms while never splitting the difference, you can create a more grounded and more critical association that truly maintains your targets and objectives. Additionally, building solid associations requires having valid and guaranteed associations with others. Make an effort not to approach sorting out as a worth-based exchange where you're solely revolved around what you can secure from others—taking everything into account, based on building genuine relationships considering normal respect, trust, and shared values. Come clean and direct about your assumptions and targets, and show authentic interest in getting to know the people you meet. Authenticity breeds trust and legitimacy, and it lays out the basis for huge and persevering associations that can maintain you all through your trip. Besides, fabricating consistent associations incorporates being liberal with your time, fitness, and resources to help other people meet their targets and objectives. Look for important opportunities to remunerate your association by offering your assistance, insight, or relationship whenever you can. Be a willing crowd and sounding board for others, giving reassurance and sponsorship when they need it most. Recognize the triumphs and achievements of your association's people and arrange your congratulations and backing for their endeavors. By being a liberal and resilient person from your association, you can support your associations and develop a culture of correspondence and normal assistance that helps generally closely involved individuals. Likewise, assembling consistent associations requires being accessible to new perspectives and experiences and embracing assortment and thought in your association. Search out relationships with individuals from different establishments, social orders, and adventures, and attract people with points of view that could differentiate from your own. Embrace the luxury and assortment of human experience, and see the value that substitute perspectives bring to your association. By developing an alternate and extensive association, you can exploit countless pieces of information, contemplations, and potential entryways that can work on your own life and work.

Chapter 9

Embracing Accountability

Holding Yourself Answerable

Viewing yourself as dependable is a fundamental part of mindfulness and achievement. It incorporates getting a sense of ownership with exercises, decisions, and results, and holding yourself to elite prerequisites of reliability, commitment, and significance. While it might be tempting to blame external factors or conditions for our lack or frustrations, certified liability requires looking inside and tracking down proactive ways of acquiring from our mistakes, proposing to sort things out when significant, and making a pass at steady improvement. Could we examine this topic further and uncover methodology for viewing yourself as dependable: One essential piece of viewing yourself as dependable is spreading out clear and reachable goals that go about as benchmarks for progress. Portray unequivocal, quantifiable, and reasonable targets that line up with your characteristics, requirements, and desires, and spread out a blueprint for achieving them. Separate your goals into additional humble or huge stages or accomplishments, and set deadlines or schedules for completing them. By characterizing clear goals and viewing yourself as liable for their satisfaction, you can stay aware of focus and energy toward your optimal outcomes. Furthermore, seeing yourself as mindful incorporates getting a sense of ownership of misunderstandings and dissatisfactions, rather than abstaining from shortcomings or thinking. Perceive when you come up short concerning your goals or presumptions, and get a feeling of pride with any slip-ups or staggers that could have added to the outcome. Instead of bothering past dissatisfactions, revolve around acquiring from them and perceiving open entryways for advancement and improvement. Use disasters as huge learning experiences that enlighten your future exercises and decisions, and spotlight on applying those guides to achieve further developed results from this point forward. Besides, viewing yourself as dependable requires encouraging a solid character, discipline, and restriction to stay on target and convinced despite interferences or temptations. Put down clear places to pause and requirements for yourself, and spread out timetables and affinities that help your targets and wants. Practice care and mind-to-eye while you're derailed by participating in approaches to acting that are counterproductive to your targets. Foster the determination and adaptability to go against second pleasure and stay zeroed in on your long objectives, regardless, when stood up to with troubles or checks in transit. Additionally, seeing yourself as capable incorporates searching for analysis and commitment from others to gain perspective on your exercises and decisions. Enclose yourself with trusted experts, guides, or companions who can give a real and significant analysis of your display and progress. Be accessible to getting analysis, regardless, while it's trying to be heard, and use it as an opportunity for self-reflection and improvement. Successfully demand input from others on how you can improve, hold yourself to a superior quality, and make changes considering their encounters and ideas. Furthermore, viewing yourself as capable requires regularly evaluating your progression and changing your procedure depending upon the situation to stay centered toward your goals. Track down an open door to think about your exercises, decisions, and results, and review whether they line up with your characteristics and requirements. Recognize areas where you could have come up short or could have improved, and encourage strategies for watching out for those weaknesses or hardships pushing ahead. Be versatile and flexible in your approach, prepared to turn or course-right as critical to staying agreed with your objectives and desires. Seeing yourself as mindful isn't just about satisfying external presumptions or responsibilities; it's connected to changing your exercises and approaches to acting based on your internal characteristics and desires. It requires significant personality care, validity, and genuineness, as well as a guarantee of consistent turns of events and improvement. In this fragment, we'll examine additional pieces of information and frameworks for seeing yourself as capable: One fundamental piece of seeing yourself as dependable is having flexibility and steadiness regardless of disasters or hardships.

Dissatisfaction is an undeniable piece of the trip toward progress, yet the way that we answer frustration at last chooses our ability to create and succeed. Instead of permitting mishaps to wreck you or deflect you from seeking after your goals, view them as entryways for learning and advancement. Foster flexibility by reevaluating frustration as information, not an unalterable quality, and by embracing the representations and pieces of information it offers. Use incidents as fuel to push you forward, instead of as obstructions to hold you down, and advance toward each new test with re-energized affirmation and optimism. Moreover, seeing yourself as capable includes being proactive in recognizing and watching out for areas where you may be coming up short concerning your goals or suppositions. Lead standard self-evaluations to survey your headway and execution and perceive any models or approaches to acting that may be baffling your success. Be direct with yourself about districts where you truly need to improve, and encourage frameworks for overcoming deterrents and making critical progress toward your targets. By taking on a proactive technique for self-assessment and improvement, you can stay before expected troubles and stay aware of power toward your optimal outcomes. Moreover, seeing yourself as mindful requires fostering an improvement viewpoint—a conviction that your abilities and understanding can be improved through effort and industriousness. Embrace challenges as any entryways for advancement and learning, rather than as threats to your certainty or expertise. View analysis as a significant commitment for advancement, rather than as investigation or judgment. Take on a "yet" outlook, seeing that you probably won't have achieved your goals or ruled explicit capacities yet, yet with commitment and effort, you can continue to progress and work after some time. By fostering an advancement viewpoint, you can connect with yourself to get a sense of ownership of advancement and improvement and to overcome any hindrances or incidents that could arise in transit. Furthermore, viewing yourself as mindful remembers fostering an internal compass and importance for your exercises and decisions. Make sense of your characteristics, requirements, and desires, and use them as guiding principles for how you want to continue with your life and seek after your goals. Change your exercises and approaches to acting based on your central convictions and long-stretch vision, and go with choices that reflect your certified self and add to your general sensation of fulfillment and satisfaction. By living with reason and deliberateness, you can see yourself as capable of a superior nature of significance and uprightness, and you can have assurance that your exercises are in line with your most significant characteristics and wants. Also, viewing yourself as dependable requires creating self-sympathy and vindication, seeing that perfection isn't possible and that mistakes are an undeniable piece of the human experience. Entertain yourself with mindfulness and understanding when you come up short in regards to your targets or commit mistakes, and battle the compulsion to partake in self-examination or self-issue. Taking everything into account, practice self-reflection and self-exculpation, perceive your humanity, embrace the opportunity for advancement, and find that slips up give. By creating self-compassion, you can develop an all the more certain and solid relationship with yourself and push toward hardships and incidents with more critical adaptability and vision.

Leveraging Accountability Partnerships

Using liability associations can be an area of strength in achieving your targets and staying centered on your obligations. An obligation assistant is someone who expects you to take responsibility for your exercises and goals, offering assistance, comfort, and useful information on the way. By uniting with someone who shares your goals and desires, you can construct your motivation, obligation, and likelihood of achievement. We ought to examine this guide top toward the base and uncover methods for using liability associations in fact: One basic benefit of liability associations is the extra motivation and backing they give. Understanding that you have someone who is depending on you to complete your obligations can serve as an area of strength for you to remain focused and prepared. Your obligation associate can offer help, acclaim your triumphs, and give a wellspring of motivation while you're feeling hindered or tempted to slow down. By helping out someone who shares your targets and objectives, you can create a sensation of connection and normal assistance that induces you toward progress. Moreover, obligation associations give a huge wellspring of analysis and perspective. Your obligation accessory can communicate encounters and perspectives that you probably won't have thought about in isolation, helping you perceive weak sides, overcome tangles, and seek additional informed decisions. They can go about being a sounding board for your viewpoints and plans, giving supportive analysis and thoughts for improvement. By using the dominance and perspective of your obligation associate, you can obtain significant pieces of information and perspectives that work on your ability to achieve your goals. Besides, obligation associations advance a sensation of shared risk and obligation. Exactly when you team up with someone to achieve a common goal, you both become capable, not solely of yourselves. This normal obligation creates a sensation of shared risk and commitment to supporting each other's thriving. You will undoubtedly totally complete your obligations when you realize that someone else is depending on you, as well as the reverse way around. By developing a sensation of shared obligation, obligation associations lay out a consistent and drawing-in environment that encourages the two assistants to make a pass at significance. Additionally, obligation associations develop liability through standard enlistments and progress invigorates Spreading out a typical musicality for correspondence and obligation enlistments grants you to watch your turn of events, acclaim your victories, and perceive any locales where you could need additional support or resources. These enrollments give an entryway to the two assistants to consider each other liable for their exercises and obligations and to give information and relief relying upon the circumstance. By staying aware of normal correspondence and obligation enrollments, you can stay on target, impelled, and mindful of your goals. What's more, obligation affiliations advance normal turns of events and improvement through shared learning and facilitated exertion. Exactly when you help out someone who shares your targets and objectives, you get the opportunity to acquire from each other's experiences, encounters, and approaches for progress. You can share resources, gadgets, and best practices that have shown feasible in your outing, and collaborate on finding creative responses for ordinary troubles. By using the total knowledge and ability of the two associates, you can accelerate your headway and gain more conspicuous headway than you can isolate. One critical piece of using liability affiliations is spreading out clear suppositions and cutoff points directly. Before leaving an obligation association, cut out an open door to discuss and agree upon the targets, objectives, and limits of the affiliation. Portray what accomplishment looks like for the two associates and spread out unambiguous estimations or accomplishments to follow progress. Make sense of every associate's positions and commitments inside the association, including how much time you will convey, how you will consider each other mindful, and what results will be set ready for failure to meet liabilities. By defining clear suspicions and restrictions from the start, you can ensure that the two assistants are changed and centered around the result of the association. Likewise, using liability associations incorporates developing straightforward correspondence between assistants. Lay out a safeguarded and consistent environment where the two assistants feel content with sharing their progression, hardships, and concerns. Stimulate straightforwardness and shortcomings, and tune in with compassion and understanding when your associate is engaging or facing hindrances. Practice full focus and posture in clarifying requests to ensure that you handle your assistant's perspective. By developing straightforward correspondence, you can build up trust and similarity inside the association and make serious areas of strength a point for participation and support. Additionally, using liability affiliations requires versatility and adaptability to oblige the creating necessities and states of the two assistants. See that life is strange, and there may be times when one associates one's necessities with changing their obligations or requirements, given unexpected hardships or entryways. Be versatile and understanding when your associates require them to change their plans or course of events, and suggest sponsorship and help depending upon the situation. Additionally, be proactive in granting any movements or challenges you may be standing up to so your assistant can offer assistance or change their suppositions similarly. By remaining versatile and adaptable, you can investigate challenges and changes together and stay aware of power toward your normal targets. Plus, using liability associations incorporates commending wins and accomplishments on the way. Cut out an open door to perceive and commend the progress you've made together, paying little mind to how little or consistent it could be. See each other's achievements and responsibilities, and propose gratitude for the assistance and backing you've gotten from your accessory. Lauding triumphs together, backing a positive approach to acting and energy, as well as strengthening the association among accessories and developing the value of the association, can foster pride and motivation that incite you forward toward fundamentally more essential achievements. Furthermore, using liability associations requires a guarantee of constant improvement and advancement. Regularly survey the ampleness of your affiliation and perceive areas where you can further develop correspondence, collaboration, or sponsorship. Demand input from your assistant on what's working honorably and what could be improved, and be accessible to make changes or refinements to your system. Look for opportunities to stretch out your association's past obligations to integrate locales, for instance, mastery building, framework organization, or personal development. By embracing an improvement mindset and an excitement to learn and change, you can ensure that your obligation association remains a critical and powerful resource for achieving your goals.

Chapter 10

Celebrating Success

Recognizing Milestones

Seeing accomplishments is a principal part of individual and mastering new development, as it licenses us to perceive our progression, acclaim our achievements, and remain convinced on our journey toward our targets. Accomplishments go about as markers of progress en route to advance, giving us indisputable verification of our turn of events and accomplishments. In this section, we'll research the meaning of seeing accomplishments and philosophies. One fundamental benefit of seeing accomplishments is that it provides us with pride and endorsement for our undertakings. Achieving an accomplishment, whether it's getting done with a job, showing up at a particular pay target, or ruling out another mastery, addresses an enormous accomplishment that ought to be commended. Seeing accomplishments licenses us to pause and consider our progression, perceiving the troublesome work, responsibility, and relentlessness that went into achieving our goals. This pride upholds our conviction and certainty, energizing us to continue to push forward toward impressively more conspicuous achievements. Moreover, seeing accomplishments develops a positive and consistent work culture by including individual and total achievements. Exactly when accomplishments are lauded and perceived inside a gathering or affiliation, it creates a sensation of family relationship and fortitude, as everyone participates in the accomplishment and feels regarded for their responsibilities. Seeing accomplishments straightforwardly upholds the meaning of collaboration and facilitated exertion, as it shows that accomplishment is a total effort that requires the responsibilities of every single closely involved individual. This uplifting criticism builds up brotherhood and association, developing a consistent and high-performing work environment. In addition, seeing accomplishments gives an entryway to reflection and learning, as it grants us the chance to review what we've accomplished, what we've understood in transit, and how we can apply those guides to future endeavors. By taking into account our achievements and the trip it took to reach them, we gain critical encounters into our resources, inadequacies, and areas for improvement. We can recognize what procedures or approaches were best in achieving our targets, as well as any obstacles or hardships we encountered in transit. This self-reflection engages us to seek out informed decisions and changes pushing ahead, extending our chances of ending up as the winner in later endeavors. Also, seeing accomplishments upholds progress toward long-stretch goals and keeps us roused and focused on the all-inclusive strategy. Long-stretch targets can now and again feel overpowering or overwhelming, especially when progress is slow or consistent. Seeing accomplishments along the way outfits us with markers of progress that differentiate our long-term goals into additional humble, more sensible advances. Each accomplishment achieved fills in as an indication of the progress we've made and the power we've used to pursue our conclusive objectives. This sensation of progress and positive advancement stimulates our motivation and affirmation to keep pushing forward, regardless, of standing up to obstacles or incidents. Furthermore, seeing accomplishments develops a culture of relentless improvement and advancement by enabling us to spread out new targets and increment current norms for ourselves. Whenever we've achieved an accomplishment, feeling a sensation of satisfaction and achievement is ordinary. Nevertheless, rather than making do with the state of affairs, seeing accomplishments convinces us to set new troubles and seek after impressively more important degrees of achievement. It rouses us to reach out past our typical scopes of commonality, investigate various roads regarding novel considerations and approaches, and have a go at significance in all that we do. By seeing accomplishments and embracing a standpoint of unending improvement, we can open our greatest limit and achieve extraordinary results in both our own and capable lives. Seeing accomplishments fills in as a mind-boggling resource for empowering a culture of appreciation and affirmation inside affiliations. By uninhibitedly perceiving and commending individuals and gathering achievements, affiliations can give everybody a much-needed boost, overhaul delegate responsibility, support an internal compass, and have a spot among laborers. Exactly when laborers feel regarded and appreciated for their responsibilities, they are more convinced, committed, and put assets into the result of the affiliation. Seeing accomplishments compensates for troublesome work and responsibility as well and urges delegates to continue to make a pass at significance and contribute their sincere endeavors to the total targets of the affiliation. Moreover, seeing accomplishments plays a crucial part in personal growth and improvement. Whether it's completing a degree, achieving a well-being objective, or showing up at a singular accomplishment in a relaxation movement or deliberate endeavor, perceiving these achievements is major for staying aware of motivation and energy toward our long-term objectives. Seeing accomplishments grants us a chance to complement our progression, contemplate our accomplishments, and reestablish our commitment to seeking after our dreams and desires. It upholds our solid character's practicality and sureness, drawing us to overcome impediments and persevere even with challenges on our journey toward individual fulfillment and accomplishment. In addition, seeing accomplishments can fundamentally influence associations and social components. Whether it's praising remembrances, celebrating enormous life-changing circumstances, or perceiving the individual accomplishments of loved ones, seeing these occasions sustains bonds, empowers affiliation, and creates a sensation of shared history and appreciation. By tracking down an open door to perceive and commend the accomplishments of others, we show our love, sponsorship, and commitment to their success and bliss. These previews of affirmation go about as any entryways to offer much appreciated, show appreciation, and expand the commitments of trust and shared respect that are central for sound and fulfilling associations. Besides, seeing accomplishments gives a critical entranceway to reflection and appreciation. Right when we postpone perceiving and applauding our achievements, we are assisted in recalling the troublesome work, assurance, and commitment that went into showing up at those accomplishments. We contemplate the hardships we've made due, the outlines we've learned, and the improvement we've experienced in transit. This reflection develops a sensation of appreciation for the significant entryways, resources, and genuinely strong organizations that have engaged us in flourishing. It assists us with recalling the meaning of adaptability, affirmation, and steadiness in achieving our targets, and supports our commitment to continued improvement and progression later on. Besides, seeing accomplishments can move and convince others to seek after their targets and objectives. Right when we straightforwardly acclaim our achievements and deal with our instances of defeating affliction, we go about as genuine models and wellsprings of inspiration for others who may be on practically identical outings. Our accomplishments display what is possible with troublesome work, affirmation, and resoluteness, and energize others to genuinely trust their actual limits and capacities. By sharing our records of wins and adaptability, we connect with others to overcome obstacles, seek after their dreams, and make a pass at importance in their own lives.

Reflecting on Achievements and Setting New Goals

Taking into account achievements and characterizing new targets is an essential practice for individual and master advancement, as it grants us the opportunity to laud our triumphs, gain from our experiences, and frame a course for continued progress and improvement. In this part, we'll research the meaning of reflection and goal setting and plunge into frameworks for using these practices. One of the essential benefits of considering achievements is that it allows an astonishing opportunity to celebrate progress and perceive the troublesome work, dedication, and persistence that went into showing up at our targets. Whether enormous or little, every achievement tends to be a basic accomplishment on our trip toward progress. By tracking down an amazing open door to consider our accomplishments, we can thrive in the sensation of satisfaction and fulfillment that goes with the understanding that our undertakings have paid off. This celebration of achievement upholds our sureness and certainty as well as develops our motivation and commitment to pursuing our desires with energy and affirmation. In addition, taking achievements into account permits us to procure huge pieces of information and models from our experiences. By examining the factors that add to our thriving—like our resources, capacities, strategies, and sincerely steady organizations—we can recognize instances of lead and dynamic that were fruitful in helping us show up at our targets. Besides, taking into account any troubles, adversities, or dissatisfactions we encountered on the way allows an astounding opportunity to perceive locales for improvement and advancement. By separating our victories and disillusionments with an essential eye, we can assemble critical encounters with our resources and deficiencies and use this data to enlighten our future exercises and decisions. Besides, taking into account the resources, open entryways, and sincerely steady organizations that enabled our success, it assists us with recalling people who have maintained us in transit—whether buddies, family, mentors, or accomplices—and the work they played in helping us with achieving our targets. Offering gratitude for the assistance and backing we've gotten not only breaks our associations and relationships with others but also develops our sensation of interconnectedness and shared reliance. By perceiving the responsibilities of others for our flourishing, we foster a sensation of benevolence and correspondence that works in our lives and updates our sensation of fulfillment and thriving. Also, considering achievements gives a foundation for spreading out new targets and objectives. By dissecting our past victories and frustrations, we can recognize areas of advancement and improvement that we want to focus on from here on out. We can use this reflection to make sense of our characteristics, requirements, and desires, and set forth new goals that line up with our vision for what's to come. Whether it's pursuing new business expected open entryways, creating associations, or overwhelming new capacities and side interests, characterizing new targets licenses us to channel our energy and focus into huge pursuits that give us delight, fulfillment, and an internal compass. Likewise, spreading out new goals gives an

Unleashing your potentials

entryway to advancement and self-divulgence. It incites us to step past our standard scopes of commonality, stretch our endpoints, and drive ourselves higher than at any time in recent memory. Characterizing forceful yet practical targets rouses us to make a pass at significance and constantly work on ourselves, both eventually and skillfully. It urges us to embrace new challenges, investigate various roads concerning different strategies, and gain from our experiences on the way. By advancing new targets and objectives, we leave on a trip of self-disclosure and improvement that broadens our perspectives, extends our perspectives, and upgrades our lives in habits we won't ever envision. Reflection on achievements fills in as a catalyst for individual and master improvement by empowering care and examination. Right when we cut out an open door to contemplate our accomplishments, we gain significant pieces of information about our resources, inadequacies, and locales for improvement. We can perceive instances of lead and acceptance that have added to our flourishing, as well as areas where we would need to change our procedures or viewpoint. This care empowers us to seek informed decisions and take deliberate action toward achieving our goals, rather than relying upon trial and error or outside endorsement. Furthermore, reflection on achievements grants us the opportunity to foster a sensation of appreciation and appreciation for the journey we've traveled and the models we've developed along the way. It assists us with recalling the preventions we've made due, the repentances we've made, and the advancement we've experienced in this manner. By offering gratitude for our achievements and the sincerely steady organizations that have helped us succeed, we empower a sensation of lowliness and interconnectedness that works on our associations and overhauls our overall success. Appreciation similarly fills in as serious areas of strength for desolate sentiments like desire, scorn, and capability, helping us keep a moving viewpoint and perspective, even despite the disaster. Moreover, reflection on achievements allows an astonishing opportunity for course correction and refinement of goals. As we assess our headway and accomplishments, we could find that our fundamental targets at absolutely no point in the future line up with our characteristics, needs, or wants. This affirmation is unquestionably not a sign of disillusionment but rather an opportunity for improvement and headway. By changing our targets to reflect our continuous circumstances and objectives, we ensure that our undertakings stay drew in and huge, and that we continue to make strides toward our optimal outcomes. This course of recalibration and refinement is principal for staying aware of energy and motivation on our journey toward progress; advancing new goals develops the support of our past achievements and prompts us toward new degrees of accomplishment and fulfillment. Exactly when we set forth forceful yet possible goals, we challenge ourselves to reach out beyond our standard scopes of commonality and tap into our greatest limits. Characterizing new goals grants us the chance to channel our energy and fixation into critical pursuits that give us joy, fulfillment, and an internal compass. Whether it's seeking one more occupation opportunity, leaving on an innovative endeavor, or creating relationships with loved ones, advancing new targets opens approaches to extra doors and experiences that upgrade our lives and expand our perspectives. Advancing new goals develops an improvement viewpoint by engaging us to embrace dissatisfaction as a trademark piece of the developing experience. Right when we set forth forceful goals, we certainly experience hindrances and incidents in transit. Rather than survey dissatisfaction as a sign of uncouthness or inadequacy, we believe it to be an opportunity for improvement and learning. Each disaster transforms into a significant model that enlightens our future exercises and decisions, helping us refine our frameworks and approaches and become more grounded despite adversity. By embracing dissatisfaction as a wandering stone to advance, we foster a mindset of constancy, strength, and relentless improvement that serves us well in all pieces of our lives.

Conclusion

As we come to the conclusion of our life-changing exploration of "Unleashing Your Potential: A Journey to Personal Mastery," I ask you to pause and consider the amazing realizations, tactics, and adventures we have all encountered. We have probed the depths of personal development and empowerment in these pages, exploring the essence of what it means to realize our greatest potential and lead fulfilling lives.

We have bravely, resolutely, and unwaveringly committed ourselves to navigating the many turns and turns of the personal mastery journey—from articulating our vision and goals to conquering procrastination and creating supportive networks. We now understand the value of a growth mentality, how to create successful daily routines, and how to be resilient in the face of challenges and disappointments.

But this is only the beginning of our trip; it doesn't finish here. Now that you have the knowledge, abilities, and motivation from this life-changing event, you can move forward on your path to empowerment and self-discovery with fresh energy and clarity. You have the ability to design the life you want, whether you're starting a new creative project, seeking a new employment opportunity, or strengthening your relationships.

Remember that every obstacle you face on your journey to self-mastery is a chance for personal development, every setback teaches you how to be resilient, and every victory is evidence of your fortitude and perseverance. With an open mind and an adventurous attitude, embrace the adventure, understanding that every step you take will bring you one step closer to the life you've always pictured.

I would like to thank you, the reader, from the bottom of my heart for coming on this journey with me. I've had the honor and privilege of assisting you in realizing your full potential, and I am motivated by your bravery, tenacity, and steadfast dedication to self-improvement and empowerment.

As you shut this book's last chapter, remember that you have the ability to design the life you've always wanted.

Accept it, make it your own, and let the world know how bright your light is. You are only at the beginning of your road toward personal mastery; may it be one of happiness, contentment, and limitless opportunities.

With sincere appreciation and best wishes for ongoing success.

www.ingramcontent.com/pod-product-compliance
Lightning Source LLC
Chambersburg PA
CBHW052211220526
45471CB00004B/1914